Will to Wonder

ANNEMARIE DE SERIERE

Will to Wonder published 2010 by Annemarie De Seriere

www.resoulutions4life.com

© Annemarie De Seriere 2010

The moral rights of the author have been asserted.

> Author: De Seriere, Annemarie.
> Title: Will to wonder : 21 jewels of knowledge : principles on the loss and recovery of power / Annemarie De Seriere.
> ISBN: 978-0-9808418-0-0
> Subjects: Self-actualization (Psychology)
> Dewey Number: 158.1

Typeset in Cronos

Cover design and layout by Luke Harris, Chameleon Design, www.chameleondesign.com.au

Edited by Jo McKee, editonline, www.editonline.com.au

Printing and quality control in China by Tingleman Publishing

Consultant, Sidhe Kin-Wilde

Dedicated to uplifting

all of humanity

 *Acknowledgements*

There are many who have knowingly and unknowingly contributed to the creation of this book. Thanks to each and every one of you …

To Chanel, thanks for shining and lighting up the world; to Daniel, thanks for uplifting others and making them laugh; to Colin, thanks for believing in me and for the love you show by choosing to walk this path together; to Gayle, thanks for the many phone conversations — your support has been endless.

To the BK Family, thanks for giving anyone the opportunity to learn and grow spiritually … you helped me find God.

To Sidhe, Jo, Luke and Alfred, thanks for the cooperation and guidance. The easy flow made working as a first time author and self publisher enjoyable. To the reader, your courage is 'Wonder-full' — thanks for your presence. To each of you who 'pushed' me onto my spiritual path, and to those who continue to encourage me to dig deeper — from the bottom of my heart I, the soul, thank you.

May we all make easy effort to change ourselves so we can change our environment and bring renewal to the world …

To Baba, your silent truth and unconditional love is intoxicating — thank you for entrusting me with this role.

 *Note to the Reader*

Some of the metaphors in this book are from
the 8 Powers of Raja Yoga Meditation,
as taught by the Brahma Kumaris.

If you have queries or would like further information regarding
the Powers in *Will to Wonder*, please contact the author at
info@resoulutions4life.com.

🖋 *Contents* 🖋

🜂 *Motivation for* **Will to Wonder** 🜂

*I*have been searching for truth as far back as I can remember — not truth that is deemed right or wrong in accordance with public opinion, social acceptances, cultural conditioning or self righteousness — but truth that is in consonance with Universal Law. Truth based on unconditional love, not love with strings attached. When you search for love and validation outside yourself, you fall prey to the dictates of others and tend to attract unwanted and often painful experiences, becoming trapped in the blaming game. Because I didn't want to play this game, I needed to reconsider my approach to life and accept that the path for truth ultimately led back to me. I realised if I wanted to see change in the world, then that change had to start with me.

I was first introduced to the teachings of the Brahma Kumaris in 1987. For eighteen months I visited their Centre in Melbourne, Australia, learning to empower myself through Raja Yoga — a powerful form of meditation and a peaceful method to recover your Powers. My first impression of the Centre was a feeling of true humility — an old house on the corner of a busy suburban intersection in Caulfield, with rows of shoes lined up under the front verandah as a sign of respect for the teachers who lived there. I'd never felt a sense of belonging before spending time with these Yogis. Still being tied in bondage to the 'drama' of life, however, I allowed myself to gradually be pulled away. Over time my practise of Raja Yoga decreased while those 'in your face' lessons of life increased.

I was getting pounded by some of these lessons and that antiquated question about life kept bouncing around in my head: what's the point? I didn't get it; I didn't 'get' the purpose of life. I remembered what the Brahma Kumaris taught me: that I am a soul; that we are all souls, each playing our own unique part in this World Drama. There is so much pressure from society to reach our highest potential, to 'succeed'. If 'success' means that the purpose of life is to simply play our roles to the best of our ability, then I get it.

In spite of this awakening, attachment to old habits and dependencies meant the integration of this knowledge into my life was a slow process. Eventually, very subtle change did begin to show. It was 2005 before I returned to the Brahma Kumaris — my spiritual family — determined to step up my spiritual development. Now my partner, Colin, and I both practise Raja Yoga Meditation on a daily basis, understanding that it is necessary for sustaining happy, harmonious relationships. That is not to say we don't get caught up in life; we do, but we are becoming spiritual athletes — though we still knock down a few of life's hurdles, we are able to clear many others. Even when we fall, we don't stay down as long because applying our Power strengthens our determination to finish the race. The tumultuous peaks and troughs that I once knew no longer have a home with me. Instead the occasional wave becomes easier to manage.

This book has been inspired by the amazing results I receive when *practising* Raja Yoga and *applying* my Powers. It has challenged me to once again step out of my comfort zone, sharing my appreciation of where we give away our Powers, and how we can reclaim them to take back control over our own life. During the writing process old 'demons' rose up to test me which, though confronting, brought an opportunity to check, change and refine my Powers. It's handy to remember that using our Power to express our virtues is what gives us value; nothing or no-one else can do that for us. When my children, Chanel and Daniel, were young, I would tell them, 'I cannot run the race for you but I'm on the sideline cheering you on.' Now I had to finish another 'race' in life. I didn't know how, but had faith that I would finish it successfully. So, no matter how high the hurdle, learn to jump higher or use your courage to find an alternative way. Never quit.

This book is based on the teachings of the Brahma Kumaris and was written out of love, aware that the Jewels of Wisdom inside each page belong to all of us. It reflects twenty-one useful steps for regaining control of your Powers to effect positive change within yourself and the world. It is my good fortune to serve you by sharing my understanding, experiences and resolution on how to apply these Powers in the arena of daily life. If you believe you are too busy to sit down and read a whole book, then picking up this book is *your* fortune. It is designed so you can pick a Power to nourish you through the day. Use it as a guide, as a reminder or a check list. Remember that these Powers are already within you; they just need to be recovered and exercised. Simply form a question in your mind about an important situation and then randomly open the book — the Power you see will be the one that needs to be activated and fostered.

Each powerful Jewel serves a different purpose and, although all link together in synergy, they each shine a different light. When we stand firmly in our Power we do not *react* to life in a disempowering way; instead we remain elevated and empowered to *act* out our roles to the best of our ability, enabling us to shine. The world is constantly changing and we need a variety of skills to cope effectively. Training your Powers and having them ever-ready is like wearing around your waist a tool belt with tools so well forged as to be revered by a Master craftsman.

As individuals, our time is calling for us to stand together as a global family. Remaining loyal to our values by exercising our Powers puts the reins of our life back in our own hands. Putting knowledge into practise means to 'walk the talk' and this is called True Experience — this is wisdom; this is success. This book is a call to action and I can only hope that it inspires you to use this information and see for yourself the powerful results, and that in turn you will share this with others. Sparking a light for one person shows the way for them to spark a light for another, creating a wave of cooperation. It is my duty to share this information. We are a global family yet we are unique individuals. We have equal right to this knowledge and we have equal responsibility to pass it on.

So if you're looking for a method to take your life back and want to create harmony in all you do, exercising these Powers *consistently* will automatically lead you there. This is your highest purpose: the life you are meant to live!

My wish is for you to recover your own Powers by restoring spiritual truth. May you find your Will to create Wonder and light the way for others.

Sweet wishes for a happy journey,
Annemarie,
October 2010

᠁ *Introduction* ᠁

POWERFUL OR POWERLESS? YOU HAVE A VOICE AND YOU HAVE A CHOICE!

Throughout the ages 'Power' has been misinterpreted, misused and abused. Power doesn't require you to have lots of money, become educated or hold a high position in the community. It does not mean you control or manipulate others. True Power is about knowing yourself so you can be flexible in life and to cooperate with others rather than to judge them. It means creating solutions instead of contributing to the escalating problems in the world. It means that my actions back my words 100% of the time, and though we may not always get this right, it's a good daily aim to have.

The breakdown of the current world system is very obvious with constant fighting all around, from war-torn countries to war-torn families. From the draining of our natural resources, created and fuelled by our insatiable greed, to the ever-increasing natural calamities. Systems around the globe are gradually but certainly breaking down. We are seeing a disconnection between young and old. All systems work the same: if there is no regular maintenance and upgrading, carelessness sets in and the system rots. Looking at our world, it doesn't take Einstein to recognise that our communication system is failing us. And how difficult it is to cooperate when we can't even remember how to communicate.

OUR VALUES

Our spiritual values are sacrificed daily in the pursuit for temporary material fulfilment, degrading an already intolerant society. We want to control the world around us and we want everything NOW! When we prioritise our core values below our material values, a ravenous increase in 'wants' before 'needs' amasses and fear, dishonesty, anxiety, anger, violence, depression and self-doubt are the result. This cumulative effect is like a pressure cooker ready to explode. Wanting our never-ending queue of desires fulfilled instantly has many of its own risks of explosion … or implosion for that matter — explosion refers to lashing out at others, while implosion refers to turning inward and lashing at myself. When is enough enough? We are each the creators of our own stories, based on what we see in the world, as we rationalise the reasons for our ever-growing demands. We have become enslaved to our own senses.

However, as an individual I do not need to be involved in being 'cooked under pressure'. It is a lifestyle choice that few of us realise we do have Power over.

Our Powers

Our virtues are the seeds of all Powers and we each possess many that give us value. How easily we forget our Jewels when we give in to conditioning and habits. Exercising my Powers puts me in the driver's seat of my life. Knowing who I am — a soul — unveils my value and enables me to use my Powers to claim my rightful success. If we do not use them, we instantly devalue ourselves. We have given our Powers away for far too long and it is time to reclaim them. When we pay attention to and strengthen our Powers, the fruit produced through applying them will be abundant and sweet.

To be able to call our Powers at will is an accurate skill that *underlines the importance* of *consistent practise* and *application* for achieving powerful results. Don't be intimidated by your own Powers — often the ones we like the least are the ones that need the most work, and these frequently turn out to be our sharpest tools. The key is to remain open and gentle with yourself. Cultivate your Powers, and you will discover a clarity regarding when and how to use them for maximum benefit. The practical proof will be seen in the undeniable changes within yourself and the world around you. As you re-introduce your Powers, you will create new experiences and become an authority over yourself. Our roles are to create these adventures individually, so it's of no use to borrow or steal them from anyone else.

OUR GIFTS

Our Powers are a gift every single one of us receives at birth. The energy of our conscious awareness is our Personal Power — our Willpower. Are you a slave to your senses or a Master of this Power? When we live a life of contradiction and compromise we waive our rights to our Powers. Daily practise of Raja Yoga Meditation helps strengthen your Powers while cleaning the windows of your intellect, which is your guide and gateway to all Powers.

To be a Master of your Powers is to create success in all you do, both in your relationships and in living a happy, harmonious life. In your hands you have a shortcut to divine insight for self change; it is up to you what you do with this information. Will you use it to *succeed*?

OUR RIGHT TO SUCCESS AND HAPPINESS

Using our Powers — our unconditional, God-Given, special gifts — creates a smooth flow. This flow gives the ability to remain stable in the midst of chaos, while lifting the burden of responsibility so you can claim your RIGHT to SUCCESS and HAPPINESS. When *using* your gifts, it would be impossible to not realise your highest potential!

These Jewels are worth their weight in gold. To use them constantly means to succeed in life. So what Jewels do you have sitting in your treasure store, collecting dust, just waiting to SHINE! Let's find out …

Do you remember your Powers?

Such an amazingly Wonderful gift.

Not using them means to take the stairs,

but to use them is like stepping into a lift.

To rise high like a shining star,

elevated high above the crowd.

Not pulled by any circumstance,

and no need to scream out loud.

Gently aspiring to being your best,

a peaceful journey, a powerful quest —

after all, we are here as royal guests,

on Earth for only a limited time —

to waste this opportunity is a crime.

So be happy and joyful, come what may,

to enjoy your Magical Earthly stay.

The 1st Jewel:

Power to be Present

True Power is complete authority over the self,

such riches are yours to endow.

Paying attention is therefore an effective key,

to play clever and never to bow

to the past or the future,

but be present, here and NOW!

ಬಿ ಬಿ ಬಿ

Presence is to stand in your Power.

WHERE ARE YOU RIGHT NOW?

'Presenteeism' is on the rise, not just in the work place but in the family home. 'Presenteeism' refers to being physically present, with the vagabond mind wandering off somewhere else — anywhere but here and now. Where is the Power in that? It is proving costly not only for employers but for millions of families across the globe. Self awareness, productivity, creativity and cooperation are taking a serious dive, while anxiety and depression are peaking at an all-time high — just look around. Anxiety is caused by the fear of what tomorrow may bring, while wanting everything today, yet often being caught in a web of the past. Depression is a deep sense of loss of the self, a loss of identity.

There are many broken families and relationships; if you look just beneath the surface you may find that 'lack of presence' had a large hand in it. Like flowers, all relationships need to be nurtured and sustained. They need constant nourishment or they die. When the excitement of any new relationship enters the 'familiar' stage, presenteeism has a way of sneaking in. When we spend too much time away from home paying for our material belongings, or because we simply just don't want to go home — only to arrive with nothing left to give or to receive — presenteeism is there. When we are busy worshipping the inanimate objects in the corner of the room, giving our full attention to our television sets and computers, presenteeism is at the forefront. Sooner or later, if we don't 'water' our relationships regularly, they wither away … with surprise being a commonly expressed emotion … 'What happened?'

Not paying attention to my attitude and not paying attention to my environment can cause a great deal of tension. Being too busy working to pay off credit cards for unnecessary baggage, re-visiting the past or racing to the future leaves no Power to make any significant changes *now*. I may even change jobs, homes, relationships or diets, then wonder why I am in a similar situation as before. What happened? Without changing myself, I carried the past into the present. It's the same 'stuff,' only different faces and different places. I have not moved on; I have moved away, neatly tucking it all in my backpack and taking it with me, too distracted to notice.

With the many noisy thoughts we invite, given a little attention it's not difficult to notice that the majority are not only negative and wasteful but are focused on past circumstances. Whether ten years, ten months, ten days or ten minutes ago, the past is gone; it's not a place we can visit except through our thoughts. So why do we recall distracting memories that offer us nothing but grief and heartache? Because many people prefer to live in nostalgia rather than move into the unknown, due to lack of Power, lack of courage and lack of presence. Presence avoids carelessness, giving courage and Power to release the past and making it possible to move smoothly into the future!

We appear to be so busy 'being responsible' for our lives that we overlook the fact that we are getting swept up in it and actually miss out on a large chunk of life. Is that being responsible or careless? Let's look at our value system for a moment. If you value your health and wellbeing, but are 'too busy' to give yourself regular time out to exercise and play, what does that tell you about your priorities? What is more important? What about saying you value your family but are 'too busy' or distracted to spend quality time with them, failing to see that they are missing out — and so are you. Many families fall apart under this stressful lifestyle as they do not recognise that their lives are full of contradictions, confusion at its core. I cannot change the past or manipulate the future, but I can change *now*. By being present *I* can change, giving me

Power to review the past and move confidently towards the future. NOW is when I give energy to a thought and have total control. Being present prevents the tendency to rush to the future while frequently looking back. When we are not present, we cannot take control of the reins of our life. Is this the example we want to lead by? Often, without us being aware of it, we are 'mentoring' others: our children, our friends, our colleagues. This natural process of leading by example is a great and humbling responsibility.

When I constantly get lost in presenteeism and find 'more important' things to do than to pay attention to life, I cannot expect to get anything done constructively and I cannot expect cooperation from others. When I'm too busy 'fighting life' I drain my Powers, like a flat battery in a torch; no matter how much you need light, if the battery is flat it will not shine! Give freely to others, but ensure that your 'tank' remains full so it overflows and others will automatically benefit.

It seems that as well as our belief system, our value system could do with a firm shake up to wake it from its comfortable slumber. The time has come for us to stop sacrificing and wasting our Powers while trying to please, impress, control or conform, busying ourselves in proving that we are good enough. We've compromised our health and relationships for far too long. We cannot change the world if we do not change ourselves. Neither can we contribute to the world when we are running on empty. So stop right *now* and appreciate all life brings you. Appreciate your health, your job, your home, your family — it may all be gone tomorrow …

So what will you do today when you know there will be no tomorrow? What will you do today when you know you cannot fail? We individually have the WILL, when using our Powers, to STOP the merry-go-round of fear and START uplifting ourselves and each other with love, to live a life of Wonder!

… now is here; let's shine together!

ACTION: Each morning, before you start your day, take just a few minutes to *breathe* and *become present*. Pay attention to your breathing … slowly in and out … notice your environment: smells, sounds, sights. Notice any feelings or thoughts without judgement. Just observe, then gently let them go. Give thanks for another chance to change and begin your day. Stop several times throughout your day … breathe … become Present ☺.

AFFIRMATION: I am a Powerful, Present soul. I pay attention to my life. I am alert, courageous and in control of my senses. Abundance flows freely all around me because I am *living life today*!

BLESSING: May you live each day with intoxication as though it were your last. To enthusiastically live and breathe life into every moment is to have connected the dots of mind … body … soul. Being an embodiment of solutions is to understand and *use* your Powers. It means to *succeed* in *life*!

The 2nd Jewel:

Power to Pack Up

To pack up we need to use our might,

ridding us of any 'excess baggage' fight.

Remaining easy for travelling light

and keeping clear our peripheral sight

frees our wings to take our flight.

ಖಖಖ

By packing up any wasteful or destructive thought,
you take the reins!

DO YOU TRAVEL LIGHT AND EASY, OR STRUGGLE WITH EXCESS BAGGAGE?

We often get bombarded by defeating thoughts — realising the implications of where my thoughts lead me, I want the ability to instantly clear any negativity that clutters my mind. Exercising your Power to Pack Up means applying a complete full stop (a firm brake) to control and direct your thoughts, giving you controlling Power. It means to travel light, to fly. When you do not entertain any limiting thoughts or carry around outlived situations, you won't be burdened or influenced by what is going on around you. Being economical with your mind creates Power to remain positive and view the world as beautiful and unlimited.

Have you ever noticed how much 'stuff' we carry around with us? I remember waiting to board an airplane when returning from a trip to India. There was lots of chaos and noise while I sat quietly observing. I had just visited Madhuban —

Brahma Kumaris Headquarters in Rajasthan — and was churning on methods for self change, when I noticed the amount of excess baggage people carried, struggled with and even paid for. I started to wonder how much of it was actually needed and how much was unnecessary waste. This baggage situation was an entertaining metaphor and a great wake up call.

Do you ever wonder why you are so tired by day's end, literally falling into bed, only to drag yourself out of it in the morning? The body may sleep, but this does not mean we receive proper rest. Nourishment and rejuvenation can not accurately take place if the mind continues to make noise — that is a two-minute recipe for stress and disease.

We cannot see what we carry in our mind. If we don't let go of stuff that has already happened, it is like carrying a permanent bag on our back and shoulders, which over time becomes excessively heavy. We start to struggle through even the simplest day and can't understand why. What about the ten kilograms of anger and resentment from a past misadventure, the nine kilograms of shame and guilt that is now permanently part of my personality and I can't imagine life without it? We try and ignore the eight kilograms of mud from digging that depressive hole that seems too difficult to get out of, and the seven kilograms of fear to let go, which is stopping us from leaving our comfort zones.

Not only do we carry this stuff around, we keep it, we store it, we hide it away and hoard it, bringing it to the surface when it fits our agenda. This load has a cumulative effect, like a pressure cooker, leaving no room for any positive and creative movement. Accumulating and becoming attached to our stuff only creates complications and we experience difficulty letting go — be it a worn out pair of shoes or a worn out relationship. The more we hang on, the more we expose ourselves, and often others, to pain. It weighs down your wings so you won't be able to fly and you won't want others to fly either. Take only the experience and travel light. Learning the lesson of letting go of everything else will propel you forward in life.

Packing up means to consistently check and change what and how you think. We have the Power to control our thoughts, to slow down the process and change their quality and direction. It will take a bit of effort as many of us have become quite complacent, not even thinking about our thinking.

Paying attention to your thoughts gives you control, it enables you to judge their speed and quality, giving you Power to discard any negative thought that has the slightest potential to create destructive behaviour — just pack them up and let them go, making room for empowering thoughts that create success. Remember, if you have built up a lot of negative in your account, it will take a bit of courage and commitment, but will be well worth the effort. To solve any problems we have created, we must first change the way we think.

When you use the Power to Pack Up, you finish any weak thoughts by applying, in effect, a full stop. Applying a complete full stop gives you clarity and strength. It doesn't mean you have no feelings or thoughts, but rather that you have the ability to quieten your mind by applying a firm brake to your thought processes, remaining peaceful and able to do what needs to be done without disruption or sabotage. To apply a full stop means you don't carry any distressing situation through your day or night, allowing you a peaceful sleep to awaken fresh for a new creative day of Wonder.

Packing Up does not mean keeping a little on the side. A useful exercise is to de-clutter on a regular basis. When my external world is cluttered, it is a sign that my mind is in disarray and therefore subjective, making clear decision making difficult. Finishing it gives you a clean work space — uncluttered for clear, rational thinking. It opens up time and creativity; it opens up life without needing to repeat anything I do not wish to repeat. It enables me to interact with others without being pulled by them or by my own weaknesses and habits.

We were born with nothing and we will leave this earth with nothing, so travelling light seems to make a whole lot of sense out of a great deal of nonsense.

Action: Pay attention. If you're feeling weighed down, check yourself. Are you inviting, entertaining or catering for any unwanted thought or habit? Brake immediately and apply a full stop. Finish it — no comma, no question, no exclamation mark. Change direction instantly, then congratulate yourself — a little transformation just took place and you are travelling lighter. Keep up the good work ☺.

Affirmation: I am a Powerful, Light soul. I travel light, taking only what is necessary and let go of everything else. I move confidently through life, free from worry. I embrace change.

Blessing: May you show courage to let go of past burdens and future insecurities and be liberated in life. Travelling light opens up many possibilities to 'fly' in all relations and interactions, with yourself and with others.

The 3rd Jewel

Power to Withdraw

The Power is to go inside

it is not meant for me to run and hide.

But to re-centre so my mind is clear,

to see through my eyes without any fear.

It conserves my energy as I recharge,

to harmonise with the world at large.

ಬಿ ಬಿ ಬಿ

Withdrawing regularly from the outside world keeps your mind free from obstacles.

INTROVERSION OR EXTROVERSION — WHICH IS MORE POWERFUL?

Our culture discourages introversion, but encourages and even admires extroversion. Extroverted behaviour is often associated with being gregarious, and usually seen as social, outgoing and friendly (yet often masks that which we do not wish others to see). Ironically this behaviour always needs an audience, and the double irony is that 'gregarious' does not mean friendly at all. The Latin origin of gregarious refers to belonging to a flock or herd. In other words, you must be part of a group and conform to group mentality to fit in. Our conditioning misleads us to believe that introversion is unfriendly, or cold, and extroversion is a good quality to display.

Extroversion is nothing more than being magnetised by what is happening around us. It wears us out as we gradually lose control over our own senses and over our life. Introversion (to withdraw), practised regularly throughout

31

the day, helps you to see clearly the dangers involved when we allow ourselves to be influenced by our environment.

If I do not retreat inwards regularly I can get stuck on an encounter that distressed me during the day. Subconsciously, I can recall that situation in my mind dozens of times. I may even feel the need to talk to others about it in an unconstructive manner, accumulating nothing but waste. Not only will this weigh heavily on others, but it will leave me exhausted. Picture the waste when we invite and entertain irrational thoughts such as — 'Why did they do …?'; 'What if I said …?'; 'If only I did …!'; 'I/they should have, could have, would have …' Just imagine all that nasty build up of resentment and anger when we try to even the score, and all in the name of what … justice? It doesn't seem to make much sense.

The Tortoise is a great symbol used for the Power to Withdraw. It comes out of its shell to do what it needs to do, but withdraws at times to rest or seek safety from danger. It withdraws back into its protective shell without being touched by the outside world. The Tortoise serves to remind us that we have the Power to come into action, using our senses, and we have the Power to withdraw. It reminds me I have the ability to connect with others through relations and interactions but, when done, I have the inner Power to withdraw from both the dictates of the outside world and those of my own senses. By becoming the observer, I am no longer pulled by any external situations and remain free from influence. This is just one stepping stone to self mastery.

Contrary to popular belief, consciously practicing introversion is a very powerful tool to effect change. To withdraw from the outside world many times throughout the day takes courage and gives strength to deal with any external situation without fluctuating or stepping off my elevated stage. Being able to disengage from negative, hurtful situations keeps us calm and unaffected. The practice of regular introversion throughout the day enables you to conserve your energy and use it wisely and economically.

We live in a world of expansive waste; if I do not use my Power to Withdraw I will not be able to conserve or charge my battery. As my battery runs low, the risk of being affected by negativity increases. The atmosphere becomes extremely influential as I get swept up in unwanted actions and reactions. I have no power and there is constant turmoil inside, no matter how calm I appear. Have you ever seen someone appear cool on the surface, and then suddenly explode like a pressure cooker? That just creates a lot of mess to clean up … better I control my mind, or others will.

Consistently journeying inward allows us to re-centre and recharge, so we are able to accept all things as they are. It slows us down, allowing us to think before we speak and to look before we leap into any kind of action. Being an observer of life does not mean sitting on the sidelines, but being clear in thought and accurate in action. There's no wasteful, unwanted behaviour, and no mess to clean up.

Being a Master of your own mind gives you stability. You will not concern yourself with waste matters. There will be harmony in your thoughts, words and actions as you become economical in all you do, opening up time and opportunities to create many Wonders in life. It puts the reins back in your own hands as you control your senses. Instead of carrying fear, you experience contentment.

ACTION: Several times throughout your day, take time to become very still as you withdraw from the external world and from your own senses, for just sixty seconds at a time. Take a deep, slow breath. Appreciate who you are and where you are … become the observer for a few moments while you allow yourself to re-charge.

AFFIRMATION: I am a Powerful, Introverting soul. I show courage by going within to re-centre and recharge. I remain unaffected by external circumstances and have the ability to interact with others in a positive, constructive manner.

BLESSING: May you remain unshakable and uninfluenced by external circumstances through regular introversion. Withdrawing is a very powerful tool to overcome any weak tendency as you become Master of your own destiny. To go deep within, drawing strength and to recharge is a gentle act of kindness for yourself and others.

The 4th Jewel

Power to Discern

When I use the Power to Discern,

I can see an authentic deal.

Like a jeweller's sharp eye,

I know from a distance what is real.

This ability keeps me moving forward,

with great enthusiasm and zeal.

ಙಙಙ

No matter how much you decorate a slimy rock,
it will still be a slimy rock.

WHO DECEIVES YOU AND HOW EASILY ARE YOU DECEIVED?

A very fine line exists between truth and falsehood. It's like looking through rose-coloured glasses or a thin veil — the picture is distorted. How do you know when someone is not being sincere? You experience a twinge of uncertainty, something doesn't feel right, a 'gut feeling'. Yet if there is a physical attraction to this person we may ignore or suppress this feeling for a while. So before taking action ask yourself, 'What do I know about this person or situation?' On the other hand, if you are the one who is not being sincere, you will probably rationalise it. When we do not allow deceit to cloud our rational mind, this world is full of Wonder.

Living in a material world, we can forgive ourselves for readily mistaking illusion for reality, but unfortunately it does bring a lot of unnecessary grief. I, the soul, rely on the physical eyes to navigate through the material world and, now permanently wearing rose-coloured glasses, my sight and therefore my boundaries have been blurred. This unclear picture is caused by an addiction to our physical senses, allowing them to dictate what we see — the physical eye sees what it *wants* to see, whereas the spiritual eye sees what it sees. If ever you find yourself in situations where you feel the need to step back to work out what is happening — what is real and what is false — your intellect is trying to get your attention. It is asking you to discriminate between the genuine and the fake. The Power of Discernment is the ability to discriminate actual truth from apparent truth, no matter how fantastic the package may appear.

Our image-driven society also dictates our behaviour. So what do you do when you are presented with a beautifully wrapped gift? (Remember that all lessons in life are gifts.) Are you immediately drawn in by the way it looks, or do you observe before you leap? We tend to get easily conned by beautiful coverings. We let our physical eyes deceive us into believing that physical beauty and physical power is worth worshipping, leaving us broken when the illusion is shattered. We all want truth but do not wish to see it until it's often too late and the damage is done. A slimy rock wrapped in a pretty bow is still a slimy rock. Do you feel angry at the person who hands you this gift, or angry at yourself for ignoring your intellect, taking the gift and allowing yourself to be deceived? Don't be angry, but remember that the truth is always out there and that sometimes we just need to check a little closer before jumping in with both feet.

If I know someone is not being real, yet I react to them on that unreal level, then who is not acting very smart? I'm the one ignoring my intellect; I'm the one sacrificing my Power. Many of us live to impress or please others, but do I have to be influenced by this? No, I don't. If I know they're not being genuine, yet waste my time conforming or criticising, what does that make me? If we compete or compare we succeed only in losing Power. To see but not see; to hear but not hear is using your Powers. Remaining elevated and sending good wishes strengthens your Power and makes space for others to be honest without fear of retribution.

To discern means to see clearly the intentions of others — what their motives are without feeling the need to expose them. To discern means to be honest and truthful in seeing my own intentions also, using what is happening around me as my mirror. Denial and ignorance are subtle signs of falsehood. I need an intellect that is clear, free from the waste and clutter of my own preconceived ideas. Otherwise it is easy to sit in judgement, forgetting my own inconsistencies and projecting them onto others, making it difficult to cut through any nonsense due to exaggerated opinions and limiting beliefs. Nonsense keeps you stuck in unwanted behaviour and afraid of leaving your comfort zone.

To be real means to be totally honest with yourself first, in such a way that you are able to look at your own reflection in the mirror without fear, judgement or shame, because you know you have nothing to hide — no impostor here. To be real means I do not create any justified action — 'everybody does it' — instead I only act through wisdom, whether anyone is watching me or not.

To discern is to have an eye like a jeweller — very sharp — able to pick in an instant and from a distance what is real and what is false. Discernment calls for me to be a jeweller in life, with a sharp eye and clear, broad intellect. Remaining detached gives you the opportunity to focus on truth. You won't waste time and energy in interactions based on lies. You will be able to see deceit approaching from ten kilometres away, no matter how nicely wrapped it is, giving you a chance to respond with love or step aside in a powerful way.

ACTION: When you notice dishonesty in someone's intentions, resist the urge to point it out or gossip about it. See but don't see, hear but don't hear. For a moment withdraw to re-centre and gain clarity, then send them good wishes. Be grateful for a sharp eye and intellect, and move on. This is a powerful method to remain free from being drawn into their web; there's no need to get caught up.

AFFIRMATION: I am a Powerful, Discerning soul. My mind is clear and my eyes are open. Because I see falsehood coming from a distance, I am able to remain compassionate, gracious and uninfluenced.

BLESSING: May you be constant in your peaceful stage so you can see through eyes of truth and hear through ears that resonate clarity. It takes a contented person to rise above dishonesty and show mercy.

The 5th Jewel:

Power to Judge

Keep the Power of good Judgement near,

it helps to weigh up with a mind that is clear.

An ability to choose while my thoughts I steer …

to enjoy a life that is free of fear.

ജ ജ ജ

Judge the accuracy of your own thoughts,
words and actions — not those of others.

DO YOU JUDGE OTHERS, OR DO YOU HAVE GOOD JUDGEMENT?

The Power to Judge means to have good judgement. It's not to judge others for what they believe, say or do, but to see where they are at with an impartial state of mind. It means keeping your intellect clear from waste to be able to assess any situation with clarity and confidence. The Power to Judge means I do not depend on others, nor do I make others depend on me. Accurate judgement happens when we use our intellect to discern between false and real, enabling us to make clear, rational decisions. Sitting in judgement of others is to deny your own intellectual ability to choose, and that comes with its own consequences.

Familiarity can be dangerous. It's a breeding ground for judgement — criticising others from our comfort zone. Throwing stones at others merely demonstrates our own insecurities and accumulated fears, which is hardly worth giving up a peaceful state over, yet we still do. Whether I'm the thrower of the stone or the receiver, neither position is ideal, as one will give sorrow and the other will take it. That's not powerful at all.

Judging others comes from a place of self righteousness — that I am better, that I know better, that I can do better. When you allow yourself to be caught up in this, you are allowing yourself to be tangled by trivia, and lose sight of your Powers. Your vision becomes fuzzy as you forget the Power of Humility from past lessons. In turn, this affects your boundaries. Besides, the company or opinion of a self-righteous person is rarely valued. Using the Powers to Withdraw and Pack Up helps you to remain detached and slows you down, giving you time to judge the quality of your own thoughts, words and actions. Ask yourself — does my attitude uplift others or bring them down? You have the Power and ability to weigh up the cost and benefit.

Good judgement also stops me from placing others on a pedestal. Let's look at the example of a teacher. If a teacher is teaching me about spirituality, does this automatically make them an expert in spirituality? Are they merely parroting others, or are they teaching by example, actually 'walking the talk'? In other words, don't blindly follow the words of others by simply accepting what they say as absolute truth. Just because someone has the title of a teacher, for instance, does not give *me* the right to place them on a pedestal.

Applying the Power to Judge and the Power to Discern helps you to weigh up accurately what others *say* with what they *do* before accepting, but without judging. This protects us from becoming self righteous while reminding us that we are all teachers and we are all students. This way we remain focused on the need to pay attention to our own behaviour. When you pay attention to your own actions, you are free to cut through any illusions quickly and accurately. You will learn the skills of making unbiased decisions while taking full responsibility for each choice you make.

When I understand and apply both the Power to Judge and the Power to Discern, I stop labouring and I no longer cause or accept any friction, nor will I waste energy getting upset about being judged by others. If I am to feel any pain, it will just be the shattering of my self-created illusions. Knowing when to use all the different Powers is to judge accurately. This Power, when used correctly, propels you forward in life. It cuts through any self deception and self doubt without the need to prove anything — you can get on with life to enjoy a peaceful, smooth ride.

ACTION: Judge the quality of your own thoughts, words and actions. Check that your thoughts and words line up with your actions. If they feel heavy and weigh you down, change them immediately. Avoid familiarity; instead of judging others, make plans to change *yourself*. Use Power of Courage to regularly take yourself out of your comfort zone.

AFFIRMATION: I am a Powerful, Accurate soul. I make clear choices and decisions and pay attention to my own attitude. I take full responsibility for my life with confidence.

BLESSING: May you be a charitable soul who judges only your own thoughts, words and actions, while donating good wishes to everyone. Having good judgement means you do not minimise anyone; instead you know to use courage to check and change yourself.

The 6th Jewel

Power to Respect

To respect all who live on Mother Earth

starts with realising what I am worth!

A radiant star, flawlessly shining,

digging deep to find my silver lining.

A sparkle of truth is that I am a soul.

Reclaiming my Powers? My ultimate goal.

ಋಋಋ

The value of a light is its brightness!

WHETHER AT HOME OR AT WORK, DO YOU FEEL VALUED? DO YOU RESPECT YOURSELF WHILE RESPECTING OTHERS?

The Power to respect requires me to re-think my value system — to ask myself what I am worth, then check that my life is equal to that. However much I believe I am worth, so I will invite people and situations into my life to confirm that. Do I value myself enough to not compromise myself, even a little? This is not to be mistaken with being inflexible in our interactions in life, but to remain loyal to our highest principles while living it. If charity starts at home, then respect surely begins with myself.

So what is self respect? It is knowing my own worth in spiritual terms, rather than the material view, and living a life accordingly. Knowing who I am — a Powerful soul — gives me infinite value and my life must reflect that. Anything less is not living up to my fullest potential, showing disrespect to myself and my Power. When I deny my virtues that are in harmony with Universal Law, when I deny these special qualities so that others will love me, I give away all I am worth. I devalue myself as I give away all my Powers. How can others respect me when I do not respect myself? When I do not value myself I cannot truly value others … and so the tug-o-war begins internally and externally.

When you look to others for valuation or validation you give them the Power to dictate the terms — no-one has power over you without your permission. To the extent that what you *believe* you are worth, others will see you in that same light and will treat you accordingly. If you spend your life running around pleasing others, no matter what you do, it will somehow never be enough.

I alone create low self worth. I cannot dismiss social and cultural conditioning that shaped my belief system, nevertheless it is *my* belief system. As an adult this external conditioning can become a comfort zone as I blame those around me for not feeling good about myself. I fall prey to repeating this pattern by setting limiting boundaries, while I live in constant fear of displeasing anyone. However resentful I may become, remaining the victim may sometimes be more appealing than standing up and take the reins back! How many of us readily admit to playing the role of a martyr, and even justify manipulation as we 'pay back' those who have misused or abused our love.

Let's now examine the flipside of low self esteem: arrogance. Superiority does not demonstrate self control but masks a different form of insecurity. Ego has many faces; inferiority and superiority are but two. When we do not live up to our highest visions of ourselves, either face will plainly show. This fear will be apparent through our actions as we recklessly try to dress it up. Thinking that I'm better than others or not good enough will nullify any possibility to improve.

Respect is knowing and valuing who I am, so I will know what makes me happy. Where there is self value there is self love, self respect and respect for others, making me 100% responsible for my own behaviour. We cannot demand respect; we must earn it. When my thoughts, words and actions are equal, respect is automatic. I begin to create healthy relationships as the Power to Respect myself enables me to sparkle and shine!

For self respect, pay attention and do only one thing at a time. Do not be concerned with what others think. Remain aware of your own highest burgeoning beauty — your innate perfection, the perfection of others and the perfection of the worldly stage — and it will be easy to flow with the current of life. Do not place yourself in a limiting box.

ACTION: Take hold of the reins of your life today by checking and changing your own thoughts, words and actions. If feeling confronted, use Power to Face. Remember, when pointing one finger of blame at an outside source, three fingers point back to you.

AFFIRMATION: I am a Powerful, Respectful soul. I sparkle and know what I am worth. I respect myself, others and Mother Earth. I value myself because I am priceless.

BLESSING: May you have the Power to renew your behaviour constantly. To check and change your thoughts, words and actions is showing respect for all. Remembering that you are a soul — a peaceful, spiritual being — generates a flow of pure love in and around you and reminds you that all are souls playing their roles.

The 7th Jewel:

Power to Tolerate

The Power is in accepting things as they are,

without giving or taking sorrow.

No matter what culture, opinion, action or choice,

do not let your brow furrow.

Loving all for what they bring to the world,

starts with ME today … not tomorrow.

කි කි කි

Tolerance is accepting all the unique differences that blend the world together.

DO YOU TOLERATE SITUATIONS OR DO YOU JUST PUT UP WITH THEM?

Like all other Powers, tolerance is a skill that needs regular sustenance. Tolerance must be put into practice to fully understand the depth of its Power. So what is tolerance? I'll tell you what it's not — it is not 'putting up with', it is not keeping score and it is not resignation. Tolerance means I accept myself and others 'as is', without exception or reason.

Understanding this contrast helps you to disengage from negative tendencies and start moving towards taking back control over your life. To accept and tolerate all situations means I understand what I can and cannot control: I cannot control how others behave, but I can control how I respond to life. What others say or do is none of my business. Accepting the choices, cultures, beliefs, opinions and actions of others without *giving* or *taking* sorrow is true tolerance.

If I get caught up on what others do or say, I give away my Power and it becomes a battle of will, caught in a rip. Instead of responding accurately I react negatively and risk drowning. When we show tolerance, we exercise our Powers by responding in a purely loving, accepting and honest way. If you think you are being tolerant yet somewhere along the line you become resentful, frustrated or even angry, saying things like, 'How much am I supposed to put up with?'; 'Why do I always have to be the tolerant one?'; 'I'm sick of being taken for granted' or 'I can't do this anymore,' then you have been quietly keeping score and may even feel justified to retaliate and blame others.

For anyone who doesn't like to 'create waves' it is very easy to convince ourselves of the need to be 'tolerant', rather than to face a challenging situation head on. That's not tolerance, that's resignation, lack of courage and 'putting up with it'. We kid ourselves into believing that it's best for all, when clearly it is not helping anyone, including ourselves. At some point — better sooner than later — courage to confront and correct the situation will be necessary. Maybe we are afraid of hurting someone or of being hurt. Maybe we fear rejection or believe we will be punished. Maybe we believe we don't deserve better. Maybe we seek approval from others or want to control them. Maybe we just don't know how to say NO.

Setting boundaries takes enormous courage and love. If you've been 'putting up with' a situation over a long period of time, you have taught others how to treat you. 'Un-teaching' them will need tolerance and courage and will only happen through consistently changing yourself. Those who are used to our 'tolerant' ways may not like this change as they are forced out of their comfort zone, that we helped build for them. We will almost certainly be challenged, after all we have been saying 'yes' for so long. So, regardless of the 'tantrums' that others may display while you serve yourself first, remember to teach only by example; not through words and never by force. You owe it to yourself, and to them, to show mutual respect. You deserve to be happy and so do they. Let go.

If you don't let go you may be compelled to 'bounce the ball back' and the blaming game will be born. When we bounce the ball back even against our own will, we become consumed by how others throw the ball. That's not using your Power, that's handing your Power to the person whose behaviour you are colluding with. Bouncing the ball back means you are taking part in creating a toxic and life-draining environment, a destructive pattern that becomes increasingly difficult to break. Saying no with a loving heart allows you to stop bouncing the ball back. Tolerance means seeing only a higher vision of yourself and others, remembering, 'when I change, the world changes'. Change is much easier when I focus on my own behaviour instead of trying to change others.

Using my Power of Tolerance is likened to a fruit tree: I remain strong and unaffected by the storms of life. A fruit tree gives fruit, even to those who pelt them with stones. As a fruit tree, if someone gives me insults or anger, I remain happy and uninfluenced. No matter how others behave towards me, instead of striking back, I am able to give them good wishes and the fruit of my experience. Tolerance is wearing a life jacket that brings success in all interactions because it allows nothing to sink my peace of mind.

ACTION: Write a list of *only good* things about someone who is challenging you and send them good wishes. They probably need it more than you. This is a very Powerful exercise. Remember, qualities we like in others are our own forgotten beautiful qualities, whereas traits we dislike in others are often ones we do not wish to see in ourselves. Be gentle with yourself ☺.

AFFIRMATION: I am a Powerful, Tolerant soul. I accept the choices and opinions of others without giving or taking sorrow. I understand and accept that we are individuals and unique. I am content and make others content.

BLESSING: May you be constantly stable in your elevated stage, remaining unaffected by outside circumstances, and so owning a peaceful mind. Accepting that we are all different and we each have something to contribute in life, no matter how small, lightens your perspective.

The 8th Jewel:

Power to be Humble

To look in the mirror with honesty

gives me a powerful ability

to remain elevated and above the crowd,

and for maximum stability.

To remain clear and never judge another …

this greatness is called Humility.

෩෩෩

> *To err is human.*
> *To learn, to accept, to apply is Humility.*

ARE YOU HONESTLY PLAYING YOUR PART TO THE BEST OF YOUR ABILITY?

Humility is another Power that appears to have been misinterpreted. Often regarded as being submissive, inferior, insignificant, weak or ordinary, humility is, however, a strength. It takes courage to face my own limitations or imperfections (the mirror test) and incredible tenacity to keep moving forward and not quit in the face of adversity. It takes tolerance to accept myself and others as we are and it takes humility to accept that what I don't like in others is probably what I need to most change in myself. It takes discipline and self respect to transform and transcend any destructive habits and limiting patterns in my life. It takes courage to let the past be past and to use today as a great day to start making even one small change. Humility teaches us it's ok to make mistakes — to learn, to review, to adjust, to 'pack it up' and finish it — without experiencing any feelings of shame or guilt.

The sign of a humble person is that they automatically receive praise because their Power is consistently on display. Their powerful status is earned through tenacious effort, not paid for in monetary terms. This is a complete contrast to being insignificant. They accept lessons in life as nourishment to grow and help others in the process, while never assuming the story of another. They will never look down on another unless they are bending over to help them up, understanding the journey at hand. They show mercy, compassion and tolerance and do not deem themselves to be experts, but rather students of life. They have the hindsight of what it takes to change, the foresight to never take things for granted, and the insight that actions claim results (The Law of Karma). Never resting on their laurels or finding blame, but always checking and changing themselves first — these are the humble.

We have completely forgotten who we are and have become subject to the turmoil of life, losing our ability to make clear choices and leaving our habits to govern how we play our roles. This is why it is so important to never judge another for the role they play. Humility has nothing to do with humiliation or abuse of Power, but everything to do with remembering who we are — peaceful souls — that we are guests on this earth and are to be a Master of our own senses. Understanding that we are all playing our part in this life drama on this world stage reminds me of the true equality that exists but has been forgotten, and is now beyond our basic comprehension.

The world is full of Wonder when we understand and use our Powers; in fact life begins to flow freely. When I learn that all I need is 'within' and that I do not need to extract this from anyone or anything external, I humbly accept and appreciate the Power we each own. Our happiness is not reliant on someone else to validate our existence, but is relative to the consistent use of our Powers. Realising the magnitude of this Power stops any inclination towards subservience or supremacy, bringing with it the understanding and acceptance of the responsibility involved.

Recognition of greatness lies in changing our perspective of the world. Viewing the world from different angles often brings clarity and identifies our beliefs that have shaped the lens through which we see the world. Looking through a different lens gives great protection against arrogance and carelessness. Whether someone gives you praise or criticism, humility keeps you from swinging between ego and self doubt. Leaving room only for love and charity, you are able to remain calm and content. When you come from an honest heart there will be no need to hide as fear has no place with you — you know your own worth and do not need to prove it.

Through regular introversion we start to remember who we are and what we are worth — valuing myself helps me to enjoy seeing others in the same light. As souls we are all shining stars but, so enslaved to our senses, we are becoming duller by the day. Understanding the magnitude of this power, one cannot help but be humbled by its intensity. It enables you to break free from the bondage of servitude to make way for true service. By honouring everyone's uniqueness and cooperating with others, we can get on with living our highest visions.

ACTION: Look closely in the mirror and ask yourself: 'Am I being honest in all my interactions?' and 'What am I worth?' While looking in the mirror, repeat the following affirmation three times. Do this exercise as often as necessary. Accept the process of making any mistake with humility and love.

AFFIRMATION: I am a Powerful, Humble soul. I see my own rich uniqueness and support it in others. I am a student of life and Master of my senses. I am worthy of respect because I come from a place of Power and Truth.

BLESSING: May you experience the true Power of Humility. Being humble takes love, discernment, courage and tolerance. To recognise others as equal to yourself — not better or worse — is taking authority over your own mind, life and destiny.

The 9th Jewel:

Power to Adjust

With Power I adjust my sails in the wind,

to help me reach my destination.

Knowing that nothing physical stays the same

prevents me from procrastination;

to accommodate others without hesitation,

is a life filled with illumination.

ಜಿ ಜಿ ಜಿ

What once was new ... must become old ...
to give way to the new ...

Do you flow smoothly and accommodate others, or do you struggle as you get swept out to sea?

Have you ever been caught in a rip? It's a frightening, stressful and absolutely exhausting experience. Imagine the ocean — ever changing ... expanding ... contracting — never the same, always moving. To see the beauty and gentleness of the ocean but remain respectfully aware of its amazing Power to destroy shows understanding of the Law of Change. This Law states that nothing will or must ever remain the same. Learning to adjust, to accommodate and to expand just like the ocean enables you to mould with any situation in a smooth and easy manner. Adjusting in life means to flow with, rather than struggle against it, just as a sailor uses the wind to bring his boat home.

In this world of matter there is tangible evidence everywhere that the Law of Change exists: what once was new must become old, yet very few are willing or able to accept this shift and hang onto possessions and positions in life no matter what the cost. We must remember that cars wear out, as do bodies. The continual rise and build up of fear is also evident. Our lack of courage keeps us from leaving our comfort zone and the consequent trials we experience are a by-product of our own resistance to change.

A great symbol used for this Power is the ocean. If rubbish is thrown in the ocean, the powerful waves just wash it back to shore, or it totally absorbs it without the slightest disturbance. When I am able to adjust in life, no matter what 'rubbish' is thrown at me, I have the ability to absorb it like the ocean or to discard it like the Powerful waves. Instead of adding rubbish to my already excessively heavy backpack I can let go of any scene without feeling the need to discuss it (gossip) with anyone else. Gossip just exacerbates the situation.

Adjusting gives the ability to accommodate the values and ideas of others, their needs and desires without compromising yourself. If someone has a weakness, it's best I not keep it in my mind in the form of frustration or arrogance. If this person is in denial of their own weakness, then accommodating them, rather than pointing it out, is an act of mercy and kindness. What gives me the right to criticise another? What gives me the right to ridicule someone else's beliefs? What right do I have to impose my opinion on anyone? Worse still, what right do I have to reduce my own value by keeping rubbish like that in my mind, to waste my success and my highest potential? I have no such right!

What I *do* have is Power over myself. Understanding and applying this knowledge is what brings success. To remain successful, it is essential to constantly upgrade outdated information in the form of limited beliefs, thoughts and ideas. If your hands are full with your own Powers, there will be no room for wasteful actions or for noticing the weakness of another. Using the Power to Adjust helps to accommodate all that is happening around us. Regardless of the atmosphere, we can mould ourselves while remaining elevated and unaffected.

Would you pay attention when walking on uneven rocky terrain, or would you walk with your head in the clouds? You would pay attention and adjust your footing to avoid slipping and hurting yourself, would you not? The more you adjust in life, the more your flexibility increases. Over time, you will be able to judge when to use courage to take action, adjusting along the way, or when to pack up and let go. Identifying the benefit in all situations generates Power to steer your life. Instead of continually being pulled back into your comfort zone by unwanted dependencies, you now have an easier method to stay on track and keep moving forward in life!

To accommodate does not require you to be a doormat for others. It means you *will* remain centred. When you are centred, the malice of others won't find a home with you. However, it takes time, patience and practice to recognise opportunities to withdraw from the outside world, to pack up your thoughts, to judge what is right and what is wrong, to cooperate with others, to face situations head-on with love and courage and to consistently adjust your 'footing' in life, so please be gentle with yourself.

It takes tolerance and courage to accommodate because, rather than being enslaved in servitude, it means to serve. Opening my heart and giving generously — regardless of how the person in front of me behaves — becomes possible because I am big as the ocean, constantly contracting (withdrawing) in silence then expanding with love. Learning to adjust myself without contradiction or compromise, to accommodate others, is a vital process.

ACTION: Mould and flow with a challenging situation. If someone is being unkind, accommodate them by sending good wishes through the mind. If you catch yourself locking onto someone else's weakness, or indulging in anger or intolerance, give yourself the same regard and adjust your footing instantly. Focus on your behaviour, not theirs — this stops you from reacting in a disempowering manner and helps you to respond accurately.

AFFIRMATION: I am a Powerful, Accommodating soul. I merge in all situations with love and acceptance. I adjust in life while remaining centred in all interactions, supporting others to do the same. I can do this because my heart is big as the ocean.

BLESSING: May you constantly be loved by all. Adjusting yourself stops you from stumbling around and tripping up in life. Accommodating your own weaknesses leaves room for development. Accommodating the weaknesses of others shows kindness — others will cooperate and aspire to be as loving.

The 10th Jewel

Power to Face

I will not know courage until I face the fear

to look it straight in the eye, brave and clear.

When fear knocks, I take the chance to face —

I open the door with silent grace …

There's nothing scary there, not even a trace.

ಋ ಋ ಋ

*Feeling afraid is **never** a reason to not step up —*
it's a chance to show your courage.

Do you let fear stop you or motivate you?

A courageous soul can face any unsettling situation head on. It takes courage to face our enemies and even more courage to face our friends and our own feelings. Developing the ability to confront and resolve any external or internal conflict helps to face obstacles in life, and can be used as a stepping stone to your triumphant landing place. Not exercising or strengthening this Power leaves you open and vulnerable, to be dominated and at the mercy of the world.

Dictionary.com describes fear as 'A distressing emotion aroused by impending danger, evil, pain, etc, whether the threat is real or imagined'. Hmmm, real or imagined … the body has a natural response to danger called the 'fight or flight response' — a rational fear where the body senses danger and the nervous system pumps us with adrenalin to get out of harm's way. I take this to mean that all other fears are irrational, based on past life events and conditioning that shaped our beliefs. If we live in a constant state of fear — real or imaginary — our adrenal glands do not get a chance to replenish and we burn out. Our bright burning light becomes a mere flicker, dimming until we are out of sight. Have you ever felt invisible?

Let's take a closer look at an example. A past event that may have impacted heavily on me — let's say as a child I was reprimanded for asking too many questions and was punished by an authority figure for 'being rude'. Growing up in a subservient environment, I feel bad and start to believe that it is wrong to seek answers and that I should just accept what I am told. I become afraid to use my voice. In time this develops into a problem as I fluctuate between shrinking and opposing. Now an adult I resent authority and abuse of power but, afraid of being punished, I let fear rule me. Rather than use my courage to respond powerfully, I rise up in defiance or shrink away. Either reaction results in me losing my Power while I allow it to dim my light. Unaware of the connecting dots from child to adult, I don't understand 'why no-one listens to me', leaving me frustrated and feeling inadequate. Using the Powers to Face and Tolerate helps overcome this issue.

When I apply courage, I am able to use the fear as leverage. In other words, our Power to Face is rather useful when afraid. Being afraid is never a good reason to not do something; to not live up to our highest purpose. Courage helps you to face these situations head-on so you can transform them. If you don't use your courage, you will under-value and possibly sabotage your life on a regular basis. If I'm not happy, it's up to me to change something. We all have Power — we just need to use it, not abuse it.

Everyone receives 'test papers' in life and has to face them at some point. If I prepare myself by practising and applying my Powers consistently, then when I am faced with a 'test' I SEE an opportunity instead of an obstacle. I SEE this fortune as a means to exercise my Powers, strengthen my value and pass a test — you know the old saying, 'use it, or lose it'. Using this Power allows you to SEE beyond difficulties to a more positive side of a situation that may seem completely hopeless. Use your strength to face and SEE the opportunity for growth and learning.

We are given such amazing Powers at birth, which we not only forget, but give away in the process of contradiction and sabotage. We do not have the right to sabotage our Powers. They are a gift, yet too often sabotage has become a habit. As we face any unwanted situation, we are given an opportunity to transcend any restrictive habit or dependency. Using this amazing Power enables us to step up regardless of the fear we experience.

'Facing' is a reminder that I only have Power over myself — no-one or nothing else. So no matter what happens, I need to face it with courage and tolerance. Old habits and situations — such as the fear of speaking up — will rise up and challenge me. That's their job. My job is to SEE the opportunity. How do I know if I have correctly applied this Power? How do I know if I have passed if I am not tested?

Life does not come to a stand still just because we do not cope. It keeps moving like the ocean, so it pays to be ever-ready in daily life. The more you face with an open, honest heart, the easier you flow with life. Whatever situation is placed before you, your Power gives you the ability to cope. When facing your own weaknesses, you can overlook the weaknesses in others and the anger aimed towards them disperses. By using the Power to Face, we no longer point the finger of blame at others. This strengthens our resolve to take responsibility for our own actions: I am *not* a victim, I am a Master.

ACTION: Pay attention to your thoughts. When you catch yourself giving in to an irrational fear, STOP ... then do the opposite. Do *not* focus on the object of your fear — focus on your courage. Remember, you can only show courage when afraid.

AFFIRMATION: I am a Powerful, Courageous soul. I use courage when I'm afraid. I SEE and TAKE opportunities that surround me. Life is abundant and carefree.

BLESSING: May you flow freely, lightly and easily with the world around you. May you face challenging situations with a positive and courageous attitude, which smooths out wrinkles in daily life. You will know the light when you have felt the dark.

The 11th Jewel:

Power of Detachment

Detachment is so powerful, it's way beyond measure;

to have it in our tool belt is a fortune and a treasure.

It does not mean being cold, unloving or unkind,

but saves our lives from getting twisted and entwined.

This Power is to love — yet able to let go,

A point of truth worth nurturing to set the world aglow.

છ છ છ

Detachment brings limitless love and fulfilment.

WHAT ATTACHMENT, DEPENDENCY, OR ADDICTION DO YOU HAND YOUR POWER TO?

Detachment is frequently viewed in a negative light, but in reality what causes you pain and limits your success is being attached to any outcome in life. We are chained to attachments, bound by dependencies, caught by attractions and numbed by distractions, but to practise detachment is rarely encouraged as it is seen as cutting yourself off from the rest of the world — to separate or disassociate. This can't be further from the truth, yet this programming keeps so many of us trapped in limited desire. It is definitely possible to be detached without 'cutting yourself off', but it takes unconditional love, courage, tolerance and selflessness to live within the context of our lives — in all our relations and interactions — with a detached outlook.

Both my children have moved interstate. I love having them around but this gives me no right to keep them here. Using my Power of Detachment, I can help them become self-motivated and self-sufficient as they claim their own wings. Attachment just complicates matters — we become dependent on one another and start to control and blame each other, which is not a freeing experience for anyone. I've seen many toxic relationships where people addictively feed off each other and the ramifications can be devastating, with each one so busy pointing the finger that they cannot see their own contributions. When I focus on a tiny splinter in the eye of another, it becomes too easy to deny or ignore the huge tree trunk sticking out of my own. Detachment means I can be genuinely happy for all the joys and successes my children create — whether I'm part of it or not. The more we let go, the more room opens up to embrace the journey of others. Disentangling ourselves to enjoy each other's company without guilt or frustration, gives us the ability to appreciate the positive attributes of others.

Attachment creates a dependency on any object of my desire. It can be as obvious as an addiction to drugs, alcohol and gambling, or as subtle as an unyielding need for people, possessions and circumstances. Being attached is like having strings tied to me that play me like a puppet, causing great fear and insecurity. Look around — there's evidence everywhere. Are you susceptible to this materialisation? If you risked losing someone you loved, your home, your job, your status, even your car or television set, would you be even slightly fearful or upset? We must therefore never judge another. The severity of the attachment will determine the addiction, and these can take many subtle forms.

We also become very attached to old habits, past relationships and past situations. We cling with such intensity — like moss to a rock — that we experience a great deal of unnecessary pain when needing to let go. Establishing new relationships without letting go of old ones is just carrying excess baggage, creating even more complicated situations that are, in most cases, doomed for failure. Often it all looks too tough, and many opt to remain within their self imposed boundaries. Familiarity, however, can quickly become a dangerous habit of its own, for the pain we experience then is the result of not wanting to let go. We become complacent but continue to point the finger elsewhere.

Detachment means to live and love freely, appreciating each moment without fear of loss — to taste, to touch, to see, to feel, to hear, without being enslaved by any of it. When I'm detached I am able to praise others instead of criticise; I cooperate instead of fight. Being detached means you are loving instead of controlling — you don't judge, you don't blame, you don't compare. Instead, you love in such a pure way that you are able to let go with enthusiasm, freeing yourself from enslavement to your own senses. Loving yourself makes it easy to love others with the same purity of thought, because recognition of everyone being equals is absolute.

To use the Power of Detachment means to SEE a positive outcome, have such clear faith that it will happen, then be able to let it go and get on with living life. Attaching myself to outcomes and other people is an instant recipe for dis-ease — of body, mind and spirit — smothering any creative and positive outcome. Detachment unlocks chains of fear and insecurity, opening up limitless possibilities.

To be 'Detached' is to live like a Lotus Flower. The Lotus has its roots deeply embedded in the murky stagnant water. Without being influenced by this environment in any way, it gently takes the nutrients from its surroundings to help it grow. No matter what is happening around the Lotus, it takes only the nutrients, nothing else. The Lotus flower is not touched by anything — even the stalk rises up and out of the water before the flower blooms. Even if it is touched by the water, the petals are coated in a waxy film for protection so the water runs off. In your life, being a 'Lotus' means to be powerfully detached, expressing only your fragrant beauty.

Action: If you're hanging on to someone or something and it's causing pain, use your Power to let go. Do not focus on what others are doing; instead focus on what *you* need to do to keep moving forward in life. This is using your Powers, not giving them away.

Affirmation: I am a Powerful, Detached soul. I love without controlling. I am able to let go of any person or situation with ease because I am courageous and have faith in myself, in God and in the world drama.

Blessing: May you remain free from obstacles and be light like an angel. To be detached takes enormous love, courage, tolerance and faith. Making the effort to become detached means to make anything complicated and difficult ... easy.

The 12th Jewel:

Power to be Silent

The Power to be Silent, an opportunity to be still.

A space to love and learn, to cultivate your will.

To go silently within is by far, without a doubt,

a chance to grow and change and to never go without.

શ શ શ

Lose control to noise or take control through Silent Power —
it's your choice …

HOW OFTEN DO YOU GIVE YOURSELF TIME OR PERMISSION TO BE QUIET?

Living in a world where we are continuously bombarded by noise means that it takes a subtle eye to notice Silent Power. Silence is priceless, but rarely recognised for its value and therefore barely practised. Many of us are addicted to and distracted by life's cacophony, and feel uncomfortable being around silence. We're used to the mindset that dictates 'the 'squeaky wheel' always gets heard'. Yet, when we give ourselves permission to experience and appreciate silence, we feel the truthful soothing of its unwavering Power.

Conditioned to the constant noise — externally and internally — we have lost sight of our true peaceful, silent nature. If we are not being pulled by the world around us, we are drowning in thousands of clamouring thoughts inside. This invasion of thoughts is wasteful, limiting and destructive. They contribute to the 'stench' in the air, which is already heavy with polluted energy. If you stop long enough, you will feel the vibration. This habit of noisy living has engulfed our original silent and peaceful state of being. Though we complain about it, the noise of public opinion or incessant chatter in our own mind is at times more welcome than silence. Why?

Because it is easier to lose control than to take control. It is easier to mouth off than to remain silent, kidding ourselves into believing we are in control, when clearly we are losing it. It is way too easy to criticise or blame others or play the role of a victim. We even justify our habits: 'I can't help it; that's the way I am.' It's no surprise people fear success more than failure — with success comes accountability. It takes courage and consistent effort to step up and to step out, to break old self-defeating patterns, to quieten down the noisy monkey mind. When there is silence inside, you can take control of your senses and steer your mind to be mindful, not mindless. Your concentration improves and your ability to make clear, rational decisions about your life is strengthened.

If someone gives you something bad like anger or an insult, do you take it and keep it? Why? Because an old habit of feeling obliged or feeling upset rears up and so we store it in the form of a bad feeling. While carrying this rubbish in my mind I will justify retaliation and rationalise becoming angry, even on behalf of someone else — so who is left distressed? Using my Power helps me to graciously rise above it and remain in pure silence … I'm not talking about giving the 'silent treatment' in return, but giving mercy by donating love and kindness only.

Remaining silent starves any feelings of anguish, so you won't need to keep this rubbish in your mind, nor will you feel the need to 'repay'. To see the weakness of another without the need to speak about it or point it out is a sign of a Powerful soul, one who speaks less and does more. Silence gives the power to lead by example only. The best donation you can give to the world right now is Silence!

Deep inside is a place of complete silence. We must first 'be' in this state of silence in order to 'do' constructively and creatively in life. Raja Yoga Meditation is a practical way to quieten the mind and re-connect with the Power within. Silence keeps me centred in my Power, like in the eye of the storm, silent and calm, cloudless and clear. Silence brings clarity to what I must do, no matter how others behave in front of me. Keeping a clean intellect is the basis of the Power of Silence so, if the eyes are the windows to the soul, it pays to keep your eyes clean and open because silence helps you to discern between art and imitation.

In silence you can reconnect and listen to your spiritual heart, enabling you to communicate effectively with others. When you're truly listening you can discern when others are being authentic, because pure love can only be found in silence. Our actions animate our thoughts: a noisy mind creates destruction, while a silent mind creates Wonder. Silence generates peaceful vibrations and governs powerful actions. No blame, no guilt … just Silence Power! To transform negative into positive using the Power of Silence is to serve the world with your mind.

ACTION: Create a daily space for silence, one minute at a time. Instead of saying or doing something destructive, withdraw into silence for a few minutes, then act constructively. Focus on strengths only; resist the urge to highlight any weaknesses either in yourself or in others.

AFFIRMATION: I am a Powerful, Silent soul. I draw strength from silence and withdraw throughout my day to replenish. I am gracious and donate good wishes to all. I create silent, peaceful vibrations wherever I go.

BLESSING: May you bathe in the Power of Silence. To give yourself this love and this time is an act of kindness for everyone. You do not need to make noise to prove your value. True spirituality shines when you do not depend on anything external to uphold your worth. Silence is absolute Power.

The 13th Jewel:

Power of Love
& Purity

Giving love from a clean honest heart,

creates Wonder for a brand new start.

As you love without agenda or fear,

the boundaries drawn are very clear.

No anger or guilt, confusion or blame …

the love you receive will be filled with the same.

ॐ ॐ ॐ

*Pure thoughts open a clear path for pure love
to bloom into life.*

WHEN YOU LOVE, DO YOU EXPECT OTHERS TO LOVE YOU BACK?

With purity of thought comes great certainty and unadulterated love — no strings attached. This elevated attitude makes it possible to love without expectation, because coming from an honest and clean heart keeps your vision clear.

We learn from an early age that love is anything but unconditional, that love has strings attached: 'I did something for you and now I want something back'. We often mistake helping others with filling our own need to feel good about ourselves, hence at times even the simplest acknowledgement, like 'thank you' will suffice. When my attitude exudes love because I feel good about myself, there will be no search for any such return. An attitude of clarity brings charity to liberate ourselves from many conditional responses.

When we expect a return, there is attachment (a condition) which ultimately leads to friction and resistance. Placing conditions on our love stifles the flow and our love becomes stingy, and when we are stingy with our love we try to control others. On the other hand, when we are starving for love we also seek a return and try to control others. When does one stop loving and start controlling? When one is not Master of their own mind and destiny. When I do not have control over myself, I place conditions on my love. It's a destructive way to live because I am attached and dependent on a return to validate me; I need confirmation that 'I did good', and proof that I am worthy.

When we give someone a gift we expect them to be happy. When they do not respond the way we would like we experience disappointment — maybe even anger or resentment — even if we deny it. Why do we get upset? Was it not a gift? If we get upset it was because this gift was attached to a desire to make someone happy. It is a Wonderful gift to want to bring joy to the world, providing we don't need restitution. Recognition of the profound difference between unconditional love — truth — and conditional love — control — helps to change our attitude, because on closer inspection we cannot deny this fine line we often cross. Once we recognise this, we take giant leaps forward in creating healthy, happy relationships. When there are no conditions there are no egos to stroke, no barriers to break down and therefore no fear.

When our vision of ourselves and others is blurred we seek a return for our love, often unconsciously. It is these 'returns' that breed expectations. How many expectations have you given birth to? Checking myself constantly helps me to recognise those moments when I stop loving and start controlling. Do you help others out of love or do you help them out of your own need to be needed? Giving pure love enables others to help themselves. If our deeper intentions are to make others dependent on us, we will complicate, compromise and even destroy our relationships on many levels.

When I do not create pure thoughts, I focus on the injustice in the world and the weaknesses of others, and struggle to let go. Being unforgiving creates a karmic account with others, binding them and causing heartache for all concerned. With pure unconditional love I can let go of my own weaknesses and those of others, opening up the world.

When I love myself enough I do not need applause. I will be able to give with a generous heart and just do what needs to be done without seeking a return, trusting that, no matter how small, it's made a difference. When we come from a pure, loving heart there is no need for social graces as actions speak for themselves.

Unconditional love is giving and taking happiness only! It means generating pure thoughts, words and actions to create loving relationships and connections. A pure attitude understands clearly the highest vision of themselves and others. A loving attitude is having good wishes and pure feelings for everyone. Giving and receiving flows smoothly both in and around us, because purity has no concept of love or fear — it just is what it is. Pure thought creates pure love and pure love blossoms when there is no agenda.

ACTION: Because actions speak louder than words, when you give something to or serve another, just do it. Don't wait around for applause; let go of any expectation. Resist talking to others about how kind you are. Check yourself ... do I carry expectation? If so, change it immediately ...

AFFIRMATION: I am a Powerful, Loving soul. I carry only the highest vision for all because my love is unconditional. I give and receive happiness and I love without expectation. I donate pure thoughts to the world.

BLESSING: May you experience unconditional love from your relations and interactions with others. When you show this sweet love to yourself first others will automatically benefit and, because you do not look for a return, it will come back to you tenfold.

The 14th Jewel:

Power of Simplicity

The beauty of Simplicity — power to feel free,

liberated from the chains that enslave me.

Compelled to please others or appease my own mind,

change starts with me, so first to myself I will be kind.

To play in the wind or by the sandy shore,

to stand in the raindrops getting drenched to the core;

to observe a child admiring a butterfly,

or sit under a bright … sparkling … starry sky …

so remember; accept and give thanks for the little things —

you'll be amazed at what Wonder life brings ☺.

ಖಖಖ

114

Even in a complicated world of chaos and compromise,
Simplicity is possible — if you want it.

HOW OFTEN DO YOU GIVE YOURSELF TIME OUT TO PLAY AND HAVE FUN?

A common attitude today is that 'bigger is better'. In Australia alone we have The BIG pineapple and BIG banana, The BIG rock and the BIG VB beer can. We have the BIG fish, BIG cow, BIG koala, BIG lobster, BIG merino, BIG prawn and the BIG Murray cod, just to name a few.

As part of losing our Power and being imprisoned by societal programming, most people equate success with having BIG bank accounts, BIG homes, BIG cars, a BIG circle of friends, BIG television sets, BIG fridges and BIG meals. A 'take what I can while I can' attitude causes greed and attachment, creating BIG expense and debt, BIG stress, anxiety, depression, anger and consequent blame … and all leading to BIG WASTE! We lose sight of the little things that once made us happy and we forget the simple joys in life.

To minimise does not mean I am somehow failing in life, it does not mean I have to do without. It simply means choosing not to accumulate unnecessary 'stuff'. Accumulation just for the sake of it is such a pompous waste and is fraught with insecurities and fear. Besides, I don't feel it is right for my children to have to clean up my mess when I die, nor should they feel obliged to keep it out of guilt or nostalgia — best I clean up my own clutter. An 'I have to have' attitude results in nothing more than a closet full of unwanted waste, adding to our already confused states of mind.

If you don't feel good about yourself you may surround yourself with many possessions to identify your worth, or position yourself as a target like a sitting duck. Recognising that I do not need possessions to prove my position in life changes my attitude and my respect for life begins to grow. Letting go and enjoying the beauty of my own simple qualities makes way for a life filled with Wonder.

The Power of Simplicity reminds me to simplify my life — to disentangle things by keeping sight of my higher purpose without all the trimmings, while showing gratitude for every moment. If I'm too busy comparing myself with others — to measure what I have or don't have, who I may or may not be, who I may or may not know — I lose perspective and am at risk of behaving in an insecure or arrogant manner, with either path leading to discordance in my life. How can we participate in the joys of life when we are caught in our own web of self deceit? When we are busy worrying about ourselves, thinking that the world owes us, we miss out. Living simply does not make you uneducated, but unlocks doors in life previously unimaginable because you remain free and open to all opportunities. It's not just simple living, but clever too.

Here is just one very simple act that gives life importance, which we often forget about or are too busy to notice — being present here and now. It asks nothing more from me than my attention. Giving someone five quality minutes of 'my time' is a precious, priceless gift. As the pace of life increases by the day and we become 'too busy', how easily we forget the importance of others as they dwindle down to the bottom of our priority list. Meanwhile, we get caught up in our own self importance to notice. Life will not wait for me! Being appreciative of all I have, willing to share with others and not being afraid of losing any of it, is what sets me free.

Taking time away from the complexity of daily challenges to enjoy nature — to appreciate life, to notice the butterfly or to sit under the starry sky — replenishes me so I remain fragrant and able to bring lightness to others. Simplicity gives life true meaning. Remembering to play is very invigorating, if only we give ourselves time and permission. Constantly telling yourself, 'I don't have time' causes a lot of unnecessary angst, so make time … today is a great day! Simplicity means life is uncomplicated and easy. If you believe you are too 'grown-up' for playing, it pays to remember that we are all children of God and we all are meant to shine.

When we give ourselves regular time out, we do not 'need' and so 'hang out' for that annual holiday. Life is what you make of it — create a tapestry in life that is filled with simply amazing things of Wonder. Keep it fun. Keep it simple. We are all Wonderful, sparkling souls. We are guests on this world stage and must treat ourselves, our planet and all other souls in accordance with this simple law.

ACTION: Commit to giving yourself regular time out to play … start with as little as an hour a week, if that is truly all you can spare, then two hours a week. Build it up to at least one day a week. Taking and appreciating your own time frees up more time to spend with loved ones to create harmonious relationships.

AFFIRMATION: I am a Powerful, Simple soul. I appreciate all the little things. I give myself regular time out to play and have the ability to give regular time to my loved ones. Life is great — I love life.

BLESSING: May you swing in super-sensuous joy, slide down the slippery slide of fun, frolic in the ocean and play in the sand, building sandcastles to the sky. May you enjoy the fragrant smell of the roses, run through the rain on bare feet and feel the sun upon your upturned face … May you simply live life …

The 15th Jewel:

Power of Patience

To be the Master of Patience

is to understand the seasons.

Recognising that everything happens

in a time, and for a reason,

enables an easy flow with life and

stops me from committing self treason.

೩೦೩೦೩೦

The fruit of Patience is succulent and ever so sweet …

DO YOU FORCE SITUATIONS OR DO YOU PATIENTLY LET THE DRAMA UNFOLD?

Patience is often seen as 'suffering with fortitude' or 'uncomplaining endurance of suffering'. But all good things come to those who wait. A gardener understands that, when planting tomato seeds, to dig them up each day to see what's happening would be fruitless. Instead, she knows she must water and feed them regularly, nurturing them while waiting patiently for the fruit to grow and ripen, and so claiming the harvest. All the while, she understands the need for persistence and acceptance of nature's own perfect clock. Many people dig up their own 'tomato plants' before the plants reach maturity, then wonder why the 'fruit' is tasteless, or why there is no fruit at all!

Waiting patiently does not mean constantly waiting around for others and being at their mercy. It doesn't mean to wait patiently for others to change, or waiting patiently for the 'right time' for me to change. To be powerfully patient we need to practise tolerance — requiring acceptance, enthusiasm, persistence and above all … LOVE … but of course anything priceless will be worth the wait. Unfortunately for us who live in Western society who are used to getting results at the push of a button, patience seems to be an unrealistic virtue reserved only for those with faith in God, or who have nothing better to do but wait.

Patience is recognising that everything has a reason and a season. When I am patient, I understand that everything and everyone has a certain part to play in this world drama — that situations and people will come in and out of my life for a time. This helps me to keep the highest expectation for people and events, without ever becoming attached to an outcome. It keeps me from getting too comfortably believing that the world revolves around me; it keeps me from becoming self absorbed, yet at the same time it keeps me from becoming a puppet to my surroundings. I'm just happy appreciating the company of others while they appreciate mine … for a season.

Patience prevents me from experiencing unnecessary heartache, because I know that I don't belong to anyone and no-one belongs to me. I do not control others nor do they control me. If someone is being dishonest, it is not my place to expose them — the Power of Patience reminds me to send them love instead, because given time they will expose themselves — it has nothing to do with me. Divine justice works whether we see it or not.

Power of Patience is taking the opportunity to enjoy the beauty that surrounds me while I wait patiently in a supermarket queue, instead of 'losing it' to 'queue rage'. Or starting a business knowing it will not bloom straight away. Understand that it will take time, effort, persistence and PATIENCE … to not just quit at the sight of the first hurdle. No, you keep working at it on your way to becoming a powerful hurdler, while at the same time remaining open for any new opportunities to move forward and grow.

Patience is a cat trying to sneak in the door. If the cat is being blocked from coming inside, it will try one way and then go around the other way, trying back and forth, but it also knows when it's fruitless to keep trying at that particular time. Instead of forcing the situation, the cat sits back to enjoy its surroundings while waiting patiently for another opportunity to sneak in. Patience is such a beautiful Power because it orders you to sit back and just 'be' as you wait for another chance — a very economical but powerful 'action' to take. The cat does not quit because it knows that at some point it will succeed!

ACTION: Practise observing life from different angles. Embrace opportunities to demonstrate patience, which allows you to open up and strengthen relationships. Remember that everything has its own special timing ...

AFFIRMATION: I am a Powerful, Patient soul. I show courage when I need to take action and patience when I need to sit back and wait, never forcing any situation. I am constantly happy because I understand that everything has its own special time and place.

BLESSING: May you find what you are looking for by remaining Powerful and Patient. Accepting that things happen for a reason and a season enables you to keep the highest view of life, never feeling weighed down but uplifted and light, making it easy to uplift others.

The 16th Jewel:

Power of Positive Thought

I am what I think I am —

therefore what I believe is true.

The Power to create positive thought

must surely then give me a clue …

a glimpse of my life that will come to pass,

if I don't change my thoughts to first class.

కుకుకు

Behind each action lives a thought.
Whatever the thought, so the destination.

WHAT THOUGHTS DO YOU READILY GREET EACH DAY — ONES THAT ARE INSTRUCTIVE OR DESTRUCTIVE?

Energy = Thoughts > Words > Actions. Our approach to life upholds our belief system, so whether we have a healthy, positive, life-affirming attitude, or an unhealthy, negative and destructive one, life confirms what we believe about ourselves and the world. In other words, what I put out there will come back to me.

Imagine being in your beautiful garden, but all you see is weeds. You get annoyed, frustrated, maybe even a little depressed about the never ending work. All you see and think about are those irritating weeds, plucking a few here and a few there. You don't even notice the beautiful flowers anymore. Guess what grows and what withers away and dies? Life is no different. Focusing on positive thoughts gives those thoughts energy and Power to grow, manifesting creations in life that are full of Wonder. Meanwhile, the negative thoughts are ignored and, over time, wither away and die. If my thoughts lead me to my destination, it stands to reason that I think happy, healthy, empowering thoughts.

Many speakers today tell us that the average person thinks somewhere around 40 000 to 60 000 thoughts per day. What's important to understand is that as souls we are conscious, thinking beings and therefore cannot stop thinking. However, as mentioned in the Power to Pack Up, we do have the Power to slow down the traffic of our thoughts, to change the quantity and their quality and to steer their direction. Quality of life relies on quality of thought. (Be aware, there are many mind mastering techniques on offer in today's market place, charging thousands of dollars. It is our right to be Master of our mind and to reclaim this right; it should not cost us a fortune).

By using the Power to Judge I can weigh up my thoughts: are they happy, healthy and life-giving or are they heavy, condemning and life-draining? No matter how slim someone is, when the mind is heavy, the body will feel like lead. It will weigh you down and you lose control, just like a little child let loose and running wild. Anger or depression is unbiased; it will creep up and attack anyone not paying attention. Like this little child, the mind needs loving guidance; it must be taught to think positively as a platform for a great start to life.

It's important to regularly check your thoughts because they *will* become your actions. Most people don't question their thoughts, but complain when life is not going their way. Many thoughts are self-defeating and destructive, but if you deny this inner conflict or are unaware of it you will most likely find an outside source to blame. If you ever wonder why things are not working for you, check the seed of your actions — your thoughts — as the problems around you are a direct result of those seeds. Behind each action lives a thought: am I thinking about what I want or what I don't want? Paying attention to my thoughts is necessary to find out what beliefs need updating, and is crucial for getting positive results.

Thought is energy and will manifest in a practical form. If I constantly think about a particular outcome, whether it be good or bad, my actions will automatically take me there! For instance, the idea of public speaking used to frighten me and stopped me from taking opportunities. However, because I was determined to succeed, I had to make effort to remove this irrational fear. The most significant Power was in checking and changing my thoughts from fearful and limiting to powerful and limitless, while creating new experiences to match them. Changing 'I am scared' to 'I am courageous', I then used my Power of Courage to book events to present talks, which reinforced my new belief. I used the fear to motivate me.

Whatever particular fear in life holds you back, you must constantly check the thoughts and beliefs lurking behind that fear and change them. Here are some clues on destructive inner language: 'I can't …'; 'I am/you are useless …'; 'It's too hard …'; 'I will never …'; 'I don't have …'; 'I can't see myself …'; 'You never …'; 'I always …'. This kind of language confirms and sustains any limiting belief about my inability to change.

Negating (moving away from) language is equally destructive, moving us away from what we want, because our constant focus is on what we don't want. Our actions will compellingly lead us to our focal point, for example, 'I never seem to lose weight'; 'I can't afford it'; or 'I never seem to have healthy relationships …'. If I don't check and change these destructive thoughts, what will most likely happen is that I remain overweight and poor and continue to attract toxic relationships. Even though I desperately want to change I will not have the Power, so will find ways to sabotage myself. Remember, whether it's rational or not, what I believe is certainly true.

Raja Yoga Meditation is one proven method to help change the quality of thought. The point is not to sit quietly in a corner with eyes closed, but to actively work with thought processes. It's a skill that needs to be applied with courage and consistency. Change is a process it doesn't happen overnight, but replacing new for old is necessary. Don't deny the old or push it away as it will come back at you with full force. Just check and change it — alter 'I don't want to be depressed' to 'I am happy and healthy.' This really is a very important point to consider and practise. It's all about re-learning until we automatically think positively again, as our natural nature once was.

Weighing up the quality of my thoughts is an extremely powerful exercise to help me overcome negative tendencies. One way to picture this is to use the Cost and Benefit Analysis (CBA) used by many business owners. What are the costs and what are the benefits of the thoughts I'm thinking? If they are going to cost me, I have the power to change them. If they are going to benefit me, I have the courage to put them into action.

ACTION: Pay attention to what you think. Use a CBA to weigh up your thoughts before putting them into action. When you catch yourself focusing on a limiting or defeating thought ... STOP IMMEDIATELY ... change the quality and the direction. Think about what you want, not you don't want.

AFFIRMATION: I am a Powerful, Positive soul. I am a thinking being. I have control over my thoughts and I can slow them down. I can change their quality and direction. I am happy, healthy and wealthy because I only think uplifting thoughts.

BLESSING: May you be a Master of your own mind. Realising that no-one can make you feel anything you do not wish to feel gives you control over your own thoughts and senses, liberating you from bondage.

The 17th Jewel

Power of Faith

Success lies in determination

to keep going, no matter what.

Continuing forward, regardless of fear,

prevents us from falling in a rut.

So no matter what others do or say,

no matter what you've heard,

remember that anything is possible,

as 'possible' is not a dirty word.

∞∞∞

Faith can move mountains —
the key is determination.

When you fall, do you get up, dust yourself off and keep going, or do you quit?

Using the Power of Faith means you put determined thought into action. It means gathering strength to jump higher and using courage to find an alternative route if necessary. It means to never quit.

Life has an interesting way of presenting us with timely lessons. While writing this book, I was diagnosed with rheumatoid arthritis. I'd been in pain for several years, which led to heart problems from the medication I had been prescribed. Old 'demons' rose up to challenge me. Although confronting, and despite wanting to quit a few times, I kept going. The process was slow and at times painful — falling several times — but I knew that if the book was going to become a tool for others to recover their Powers, I had to get up every single time. Quitting was not an option. I recognised my own inconsistencies and stepped up the application of my own Powers to stop me from fluctuating and falling back into old patterns.

When you keep faith, determination lends a hand. It helps you to let go and dare to *do*, while fear steps aside because courage has arrived. No matter what, just KEEP GOING ... even if you fall ten times, get up eleven, twelve, thirteen times. Feeling hopeless is negative and has its own destructive consequences: we will not be able to access our inner spark and can therefore not light the way for others. As we are individually responsible for our own transformation, never think 'It's too hard'; 'I'm too old'; 'It's too late!' Worse still, don't wait for others to change. Let faith guide you, let courage support you and let your positive thinking take expressive shape in your life.

Having faith in myself means having trust in my own experiences and showing courage to experiment. It's about determination to do what needs to be done, without dependence on or worshipping any external support. If I blindly place my trust in things or senselessly follow others, maybe even place them on a pedestal, when that trust is broken, my faith begins to crumble. Life is too short for doubts as, given the slightest chance, they will betray us. At the very least they distort the truth and cause distrust, fear, insecurity, confusion and reluctance.

Faith gives you determination to keep going. Faith gives you courage to find different ways to LIVE life. Faith gives you infinite enthusiasm to successfully finish any projects you start. When there is pure thought in my mind and pure love in my heart, I have the ability to let go of the outcome, leaving no room for ambivalence. When I have faith that victory is guaranteed, there are no doubts and success will come.

Faith is like a Sword in the making — there are many ways to forge a sword, but the basic principle applies to them all. It is hammered into shape while being dipped in fire and cold water many times, each time gaining strength. It needs cutting, grinding and filing until it reaches perfection. So when those times in life arise where you feel 'beaten' … when you tell yourself 'it's all too hard' … when you *believe* 'I can't do it' … what do you do? Do you quit, get angry or upset, make excuses or look for an outside source to blame? Or do you learn, grow, change and get up eleven times?

Faith means I must commit myself to whatever task I take on in life. Imagine a climber wishing to conquer Mt Everest with a 'we will see' attitude. Not only would they most likely fail, but they may also injure themselves in the process. If they wish to succeed they know, like any successful athlete, that they must commit, be courageous and be consistent in their practise and preparation. They know that if they are to be victorious, they must have full faith in themselves that they will succeed, while letting go of the outcome. If it's not in their fortune to succeed at that time, they know they gave it their best … they learn, grow, change and 'get up eleven times'. Not for a moment do they doubt their own ability, but each time they have full faith in victory as they move towards the next opportunity.

ACTION: At the start of any new project, visualise a successful outcome. Do something each day, no matter how small, towards that outcome, keeping a firm eye on your goal. Trust that the outcome will be successful and let go. Combined with Faith, use the Power of Positive Thought and the Power to Face.

AFFIRMATION: I am a Powerful, Faithful soul. I am courageous and victorious — success is my birthright. I am tenacious in thought and action, and trust that benefit comes automatically.

BLESSING: May you be fearless and rise up to take opportunities for success. Having true faith means understanding the task at hand and letting courage be your guide. It means already experiencing victorious elation while stepping up towards the peak of the mountain with absolute certainty of success.

The 18th Jewel:

Power of Compassion

To humbly soothe the pain of another

by letting them know you are there,

with practical help or a hold of their hand,

can demonstrate how much you care.

Yet suffer you not, as compassion is such —

A strong, open heart with a gentle touch.

ಇ ಇ ಇ

*Compassion is the synergy
of all our Powers.*

How do you alleviate the pain of another without oppressing your own Powers?

Compassion is another Power that has a load on it. What does compassion actually mean? Is it to take away another's pain by taking over? Is that not control? Is it to suffer in order to help another? Is that not martyrdom?

Compassion knows each journey has many twists in the road and that some lead to quicksand. If someone is sinking in quicksand, would it show compassion or foolishness to jump in and try to save them? Compassion brings courage and cooperation to remain on solid ground while throwing a rope for support. It brings discernment and tolerance to recognise *their* choice to grab hold of the rope, or not. It also brings love, detachment and good judgement to not be persuaded to jump in, but to use our Powers to do our best to enable the best outcome for everyone.

Compassion is a strong desire to alleviate the suffering of another, but is at times associated with 'co-suffering'. That's a distorted view, but held by many. True compassion does not mean I should endure any pain (or guilt) in order to ease the affliction of another. It means to give or take kindness only — not to jump in the quicksand. Sometimes we feel guilty because someone is suffering more than us, so we may 'put up with' a situation, confusing this gesture with compassion. Our 'polite' conditioning tells us that to not show some guilt would render you aloof and non-caring. This is so far removed from the truth. How can a Paramedic do their job if they become even slightly emotional? Compassion is to support and care for others as you would like them to support and care for you, with no question or judgement.

Most of my life, personally and professionally, I have had the privilege of being in the company of people with diverse backgrounds, many with a multiplicity of needs, ranging from low to high support. Compassion is to cooperate with anyone in need of support — without taking away their right or enforcing our right — while acting as loving guardian of our own safety and wellbeing. It means I do not take over to write their story, nor do I sacrifice my own — helping others at the expense of your own health and wellbeing is to oppress or sacrifice your own Powers. I compromised my Powers many times in life by placing my own needs at the bottom of the list and, at times, jumping into the quicksand with others — to my detriment.

Like any action, suppressing your own Powers has consequences. I live with chronic pain as a result, having experienced bouts of anxiety and depression. However, I take full responsibility for my actions and live with no regrets. I have learnt so much about my Powers and what's come to light for me is this: if I'm a soul playing a role, I then have the Power to change and play other roles. This recognition inspires me to choose a healthy, happy role. I've come to understand the vast difference between service and servitude, and realise that subservience serves no-one. I have a better understanding and ability to identify the line between compassion and martyrdom, which stops me from crossing it.

Recognising the importance of self love gives a clearer picture of self responsibility. I understand and accept the special timing of my reduced mobility and use this karma as a constant reminder to *use* my Powers. When we are too busy helping others and we ignore signals to slow down, we're giving away our Powers, because we deny ourselves the same right of care. Compassion needs courage to ensure you are not taking sorrow, as otherwise you are at risk of injury, burnout and illness. Not treating ourselves as equal to others means there is lack of self respect, resulting in self sabotage — that is not compassion or service, that is servitude. To remain constructive in any circumstance, we must apply the first rule of first aid — take care of our own safety and wellbeing first. After all, charity does begin at home.

When I am compassionate I recognise that we have equal rights and I act in line with that. If I don't make effort to slow down and transform old habits of placing myself at the bottom of the list, the drama in life will find a way to do it for me. Often, if we don't pay attention, it forces us to slow down to find an alternative way to live. When we run out of reasons for our unwillingness to change, we will be challenged to transform ourselves. To see this as a blessing rather than an inconvenience opens up new and wondrous opportunities. I now see an opportunity to educate others on self love, self respect and self care.

Compassion is humble. Compassion knows that no two life stories will be identical, no matter how similar. Compassion does not assume what you would do given the same situation — an area where judgement often takes place. Compassion brings love, cooperation and generosity from a big heart to create a healing environment without any feelings of obligation. You can never truly know what another is thinking or where they are coming from. To be generous with our heart, rather than our pocket, is compassion. It helps me to put aside 'my stuff' for a while so others may benefit. This is not to be mistaken with 'co-suffering'. Instead, keep a cool head and a calm, gentle disposition. It means I'm not scared of getting my hands dirty to help another.

ACTION: Pay attention to your actions when offering help. Check: 1. Am I taking away their right by taking over? 2. Am I enforcing my right? 3. Am I sacrificing my Powers? STOP immediately. Change your attitude to one of self-love and cooperation.

AFFIRMATION: I am a Powerful, Compassionate soul. I ensure my own safety and wellbeing while supporting others to help themselves. I know we each have our own story and do not judge. I listen patiently and act generously.

BLESSING: May you have the wisdom to understand the difference between compassion, control and martyrdom. There is a very fine line that many cross in their pursuit to help others. We help no-one when we help others out of our own need to be needed. Be merciful, starting with yourself.

The 19th Jewel:

Power to Cooperate

If we can each lift just one finger,

imagine the magic we can create.

Sharing our strengths to help each other

is such a loving way to donate.

There's no need to walk a crooked line,

when we can reach our destination straight.

ಋ ಋ ಋ

Cooperation = mutual effort, leading to mutual benefit.

WHAT DO YOU SEE IN OTHERS — THEIR STRENGTHS OR THEIR WEAKNESSES?

Having a purpose, whether you think of it as an aim or a vision, lights our inner fire and motivates us on the deepest level. Being unclear about our individual purpose — in life, in relationships, in daily interactions with others, or within a group or organisation — will make it difficult to come together and work out a collective purpose. Everyone is pulling in different directions, each of us failing to recognise our own unique importance within any group, and conflict occurs.

We all have something to contribute in life, though often we are too caught up in it to notice or even appreciate it. When we see our own unique abilities, we more readily see the specialities in others. It's truly *seeing* each other; seeing our special gifts, no matter how small. Even the grandest 'machine' will be dysfunctional if the tiniest screw is missing. Understanding this liberates us from the fluctuation of feeling superior or inferior to others and frees us from any subsequent blame, justification or condescending attitudes toward others.

Cooperation combines our individual strengths for a shared purpose. It is mutual effort leading to mutual benefit. However, effort is often associated with hard work. For instance, if I am in need of exercise but see it as labour, will it be easy or difficult? Breaking down the word effort — ef = effect and fort = strength — to use own strength to effect change, shows a new significance. When we cooperate, we combine all our strengths to effect change. We're invited to evaluate our own thoughts, our own words, our own actions. It underlines responsibility for the self, through self motivation and discipline, to stop unwanted behaviour. Cooperation works with what we have, not battling with what we don't have. It's a synergy of individuals working together for a greater cause.

If we look at our fingers, we know they are all separate, yet they work together for mutual benefit. They do not compete or bring each other down. Sometimes we are so self-absorbed in our own little world that nothing else exists. We cannot each move a mountain on our own, but we *can* move it together. We have a basic need to sort out our own personal relations, which is possible through practising the art of cooperation.

It does take courage to facilitate cooperation as others may use you as target practice to judge or blame, to criticise or debase, so the importance of self respect is also emphasised. When you remain constantly elevated you experience self respect, your stage will not fluctuate and you will therefore not be influenced by the limiting thoughts of others. This is a Wonderfully rich environment for all to grow and change. Ego is surrendered and competition is laid to rest. A feeling of union is experienced by all.

Being cooperative shows kindness combined with mutual respect. It keeps us easy in each other's company, accepting of the difference in cultures, religions or opinions, while enjoying our own individuality. It makes moving forward as a united team smooth and simple, as we trust, support and encourage each other to succeed. Cooperation brings out the best in all of us and leads us to our highest purpose together. It's Learning > Growing > Changing > Teaching > Learning > Growing > Changing > Teaching > Learning ... it's constantly working on myself in order to unite with others, becoming sweet in nature because everyone loves a fragrant flower. In union there is strength, but division makes us fall.

ACTION : If you find yourself being intolerant and focusing on a weakness of another, keep your stage stable by having pure and positive thoughts for them. Use your Power to Adjust and accommodate them by using your own strengths to help them find theirs. Encourage and uplift them to succeed in their purpose — don't bring them down by pointing out their weakness, but help them find their speciality.

AFFIRMATION: I am a Powerful, Cooperative soul. I know my purpose and donate my strengths for the benefit of others. I uphold my own value while supporting others to succeed.

BLESSING: May you be a cooperative soul who helps others soar like eagles and may you receive support from everyone. When each lifts one finger of help there is a feeling of lightness and harmony. Everyone feels good about their contribution and situations flow smoothly, as each helps the other create their own masterpiece in life.

The 20th Jewel:

Power of Realisation

When I realise that it's up to me,

that no-one else can set me FREE;

that I must firstly to myself be kind,

to set about and change my mind,

I'm humbled by the Power inside.

My eyes, now open large and wide —

upon this awareness I must act

to deliver the most abundant impact.

ಖ ಖ ಖ

To realise is greatness, to act upon realisation is divine ...

What is an 'aha' moment and what do you do after an 'aha' moment?

We all have limitless potential, but very few live up to it or are even aware of it. Why dig for gold if you don't know you're sitting right on top of it? Once we do realise where the treasure is, however, we must make effort to dig if we are to benefit.

So what is realisation? It is that 'aha' moment, that surge of energy, that 'light switch' that has just been turned on. It's that moment of clarity where you gain wisdom (insight) which has come to teach you something about yourself, and can be used to change your life. So what do you do after an 'aha' moment? To do nothing would be a waste. To ignore an opportunity to stay in your comfort zone would also be a loss. With realisation comes the responsibility to act.

The Power of Realisation only becomes Powerful when you take new information and bring it into your life — to act on it. This helps to gently let go of the old. Taking action confirms the clarity of understanding and solidifies your upgraded belief. If you do not act after realisation, your Power to change diminishes and you risk reverting to old habits and addictions. If you do not regularly review and revise your actions, your life experiences will reflect your lack of growth.

To make this shift even more powerful is to share the lessons you learn with others, giving them practical tools for ease of digging for their own treasures. Giving them space to find out what works and what doesn't supports them to experiment on their own terms and in their own time. This is one method of doing service, giving back for the greater good of all. A sign of you using the Power to Realise is that others are able to experience the intoxication of awareness through your practical form — through your vibration and your attitude.

For me, the realisation that I'm a soul with Powers and that my body animates my thoughts has motivated me to dig for my Powers. It's like an arrow on a treasure map pointing to a spot that says 'dig here' — my enthusiasm returns as one by one I recover my spiritual gifts. Naturally, challenges will come —

that's life. These opportunities come to test your understanding and accurate application of your Powers. Like any test, you can study and prepare yourself so when they arrive you can pass and take the elevator of life. Otherwise you may need to labour and take the stairs … or you can choose to do nothing and fail. The more effort you make to dig for your Powers and use them, the more they help navigate you through the plethora of choice and belief, giving you the means to pass any test. It's a pre-requisite for harmony and abundance.

Recognising that no-one can upset me without my approval is another 'aha' moment — the moment when I realise that truth starts with me. Realising that I actually have control over my life, providing I use my Powers, helps me to become an instrument for change. It is our duty to remove the shackles of guilt, shame and self doubt, as well as ego and arrogance, to open doors that until now we haven't imagined possible. When I realise that I have inside me all the Powers I need to live a successful, fulfilled life, and that I have the Power to change the world, I am humbled. Life starts to dance to the tune of my happy vibration, encouraging me to learn to be more effective in using my Powers. To realise that your success is not reliant on the outside world — in fact understanding that external success in all you do is reliant on your recognition of and applying your inner Powers — motivates you to dig for your own jewels.

Upon understanding our Powers, we recognise the level of responsibility to use them — to be serious in our attitude towards self exploration and learning, yet sweet and easy in our natural merciful state toward ourselves and others. This is compassion in its highest form. A strong seed that creates a strong tree is proof of a powerful seed blooming into its own full expression.

ACTION: Give yourself a moment to reflect and figure out a plan of action when adorned with an 'aha' moment, then take steps to materialise this realisation. Don't wait for that 'perfect' moment — starting anywhere is a good place. No matter how small the step, just keep going — don't look back.

AFFIRMATION: I am a Powerful, Self-Actualising soul. I realise I have many Powers. It is up to me to use my Powers to reach my highest potential, and guide and support others to reach theirs. Life is Wonderful!

BLESSING: May you realise your highest vision in life and recognise the highest vision of others. To move upward and onward to the peak of the mountain is an epic journey, but one to be thoroughly enjoyed as you stand in vast freedom and the immense beauty of possibility.

The 21st Jewel:

Power of Enthusiasm

Anything is possible with Enthusiasm,

it brings joy to you and me.

It lightens up our heavy load,

while charging up our energy.

We can fly high through the clear sky,

like a bouncing, bright kite.

Or play like innocent children,

as we laugh with pure delight.

ಖ ಖ ಖ

The vibration of Enthusiasm spreads
like the fragrance of a rose.

How do you view the world? Do you see opportunities or obstacles?

Our social structures teach us we must be passionate in life to prove the extent of our commitment. Passion may push us to attain our goals, but can also dictate the cost. In other words, some will do anything in their pursuit for success, compromising and sacrificing their core values, their relationships and even their own health in the name of passion. They create their own web and get caught in it. They stop paying attention to what's important and, rather than creating a good atmosphere, cause tension instead.

Enthusiasm, on the other hand, means to be filled with divine energy. It comes from the ancient Greek word 'enthousiasmos' meaning 'the god within'. When we tap this essence and allow it to flow through us into the world, uninterrupted and for free, we experience the feeling of enthusiasm. It's connecting to our inner

Power and bringing energy and excitement to all we do — a feeling of being truly alive and accepting that everything in the world drama is as it should be. Enthusiasm accepts what is and what is not, and sparks that fire in our belly each single day to get out of bed in the morning. It's our attitude that creates our atmosphere, through our vibrations. Our attitude is the foundation of our atmosphere. If the seed is powerful, the tree will bloom.

Of course there is nothing wrong with passion when used constructively. Passion can light our motivation and get us moving, but if we become careless and lose attention it can stir up intense emotion, causing attachment and tension. We can very quickly lose sight as it steers us off our intended path. While enthusiasm is infectious, its fragrance spreads like that of a rose and can be captivating, sparking re*soul*ution. It helps us reach our highest destination, as without it we only find excuses. It makes us aware of the effort involved to succeed, but finds ways to keep it interesting and fun. Most people can't help but respond positively when greeted with enthusiasm, it supports faith and encourages cooperation, usually leading to a successful outcome. And, if not, enthusiasm gives you fortitude to keep trying.

Still, enthusiasm also reminds you that you cannot please everyone, so don't let anyone diminish your joy. Some will try, but if you let them you can't blame them. Some people pretend to enjoy misery and will react aversively to 'happiness' — that's their choice. When we allow ourselves to get trapped in the influence of others, we are unable to see our own goodness — or theirs — their negativity becomes stronger than our enthusiasm and once again we give away our Powers. We let their heaviness weigh us down and we cannot shine, stopping ourselves from giving light. Focus on your Powers, not others' negativity, and send them love. They probably really need it.

Enthusiasm helps you to see any obstacle as an opportunity. Do you *see opportunities* or *obstacles?* Life is filled with endless opportunities, but only if we choose to see and take them. Have you ever been in a situation where not only did you SEE the obstacle, but you actually picked it up and stuck it in your already too-heavy backpack? I know I have — unconsciously in auto-drive at the time. So it pays to do a little investigation into our mind and ask it, how do I view the world? Do I see and take the opportunities, or does my stage fluctuate upon seeing obstacles? Do I become influenced by them and let my joy dissipate? What do I do about it?

When I integrate the lessons from the past and use them NOW, it gives me strength, courage, Power and motivation to keep going. When I become the sword, and cut through any negative illusions, thoughts, beliefs or attitudes,

I can get on with what is beneficial for myself and others in an enthusiastic way. I learn to accept and tolerate what I can and cannot control and take responsibility for how I choose to respond to any situation. I reclaim my Power because faith keeps me enthusiastic and turns mountains into molehills. To experience life to the fullest and *see* positive, powerful outcomes is enthusiasm. It means to be light and easy in your approach to life and to see all things like the first time. It's the innocence of a child.

When we need to labour for anything, we are working against our Powers rather than with them. Without enthusiasm we feel our efforts more; with it grace flows easily. The happiness in your eyes and face can help remove sorrow for many — so smile with enthusiasm … it is light and it is free. Enthusiasm draws you out of the past and into the present. Enjoying NOW creates a Wonderful future! This is using your zeal and enthusiasm for a better world. This is Power.

ACTION: When undertaking any task, check yourself to see if you are remaining light. If you are feeling tired or heavy, apply a brake and withdraw to recharge your battery for a few moments. Check to see if your thoughts and attitude need changing — if so, do so NOW. Apply enthusiasm to every task.

AFFIRMATION: I am a Powerful, Enthusiastic soul. I remain free from influence as I overflow with abundance. I use my energy economically and wisely to stay light, easy and above the crowd. I have fun and only see positive outcomes. Life is a joy.

BLESSING: May you remain filled with divine energy that overflows like the fragrance of a rose. It takes a great soul to pay attention to their own thoughts and attitudes, using their wisdom to change any kind of inner defeatism. An Enthusiastic soul has the ability to remain elevated above the crowd and lift others up.

The time is here, the time is NOW,

no longer will we need to bow

or lower our heads in emotional shame!

So stand in your Power, no need to blame,

this worldly play is a WONDERFUL game,

just SPARKLE so others can do the same …

No more fighting for 'yours' and 'mine',

is an attitude that's purely divine.

It is time to let go …

IT IS TIME TO SHINE!

Notes

Notes

❦ Notes ❦

Notes

✿ *About the Brahma Kumaris* ✿

The Brahma Kumaris World Spiritual University is a non-profit organisation with over 8 500 centres in over one hundred countries. With headquarters on India's Mt Abu, Rajasthan, the global organisation currently hosts over 800 000 regular students at the various Centres, with students striving to live a life of elevated principles. Underlying the teaching of the Brahma Kumaris is the aim to be living examples of cooperation, while showing others how to serve the world.

While the Brahma Kumaris teaches many principles for a happy, harmonious life, I'd like to list four in particular:

ও when I change, the world changes;

ও give no sorrow, take no sorrow;

ও our attitude creates vibrations that shape our environment, and

ও never be arrogant as to look down on others, bend and be flexible to help uplift them

The Brahma Kumaris strive each day to promote self awareness, self respect, respect for others and respect for the planet. The Raja Yoga Centres run on voluntary contributions and offer many free courses for self improvement. To learn more about the organisation or to book a course, please visit the following websites:

Worldwide: **www.bkwsu.org**

In Australia: **bkwsu.org/au**

🌀 *Brahma Kumaris* 🌀

For your nearest Raja Yoga Centre in Australia, please contact the main centres below:

Brisbane
347 Milton Road
Auchenflower QLD 4066
T 61-7-3368 2391
E **brisbane@au.bkwsu.org**

Melbourne
256 Brunswick Street
Fitzroy VIC 3065
T 61-3-9417 4883
E **fitzroy@au.bkwsu.org**

Perth
2 Excelsior St
Shenton Park WA 6008
T 61-8-9388 6101
E **perth@au.bkwsu.org**

Hobart
51 Risdon Road
New Town TAS 7008
T 61-3-6278 3788
E **hobart@au.bkwsu.org**

Sydney – main centre
78 Alt Street
Ashfield NSW 2131
T 61-2-9716 7066
E **sydney@au.bkwsu.org**

Canberra
38 Wisdom Street
Hughes ACT 2605
T 61-2-6260 5525
E **canberra@au.bkwsu.org**

Adelaide
414 Portrush Road
Linden Park SA 5065
T 61-8-8338 4531
E **adelaide@au.bkwsu.org**